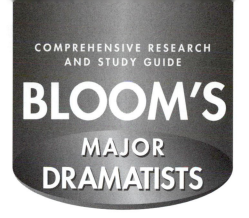

COMPREHENSIVE RESEARCH
AND STUDY GUIDE

# BLOOM'S
## MAJOR
## DRAMATISTS

*Aristophanes*

EDITED AND WITH AN
INTRODUCTION BY HAROLD BLOOM

## BLOOM'S MAJOR DRAMATISTS

Aeschylus

Anton Chekhov

Aristophanes

Berthold Brecht

Euripides

Henrik Ibsen

Ben Johnson

Christopher Marlowe

Arthur Miller

Eugene O'Neill

Shakespeare's Comedies

Shakespeare's Histories

Shakespeare's Romances

Shakespeare's Tragedies

George Bernard Shaw

Neil Simon

Sophocles

Tennessee Williams

August Wilson

## BLOOM'S MAJOR NOVELISTS

Jane Austen

The Brontës

Willa Cather

Stephen Crane

Charles Dickens

Fyodor Dostoevsky

William Faulkner

F. Scott Fitzgerald

Thomas Hardy

Nathaniel Hawthorne

Ernest Hemingway

Henry James

James Joyce

D. H. Lawrence

Toni Morrison

John Steinbeck

Stendhal

Leo Tolstoy

Mark Twain

Alice Walker

Edith Wharton

Virginia Woolf

## BLOOM'S MAJOR WORLD POETS

Geoffrey Chaucer

Emily Dickinson

John Donne

T. S. Eliot

Robert Frost

Langston Hughes

John Milton

Edgar Allan Poe

Shakespeare's Poems & Sonnets

Alfred, Lord Tennyson

Walt Whitman

William Wordsworth

## BLOOM'S MAJOR SHORT STORY WRITERS

William Faulkner

F. Scott Fitzgerald

Ernest Hemingway

O. Henry

James Joyce

Herman Melville

Flannery O'Connor

Edgar Allan Poe

J. D. Salinger

John Steinbeck

Mark Twain

Eudora Welty

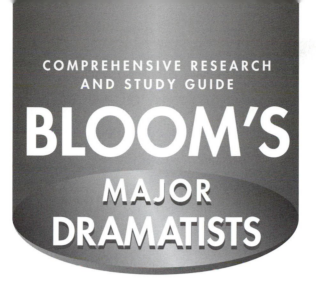

COMPREHENSIVE RESEARCH
AND STUDY GUIDE

# BLOOM'S
## MAJOR
## DRAMATISTS

# *Aristophanes*

CPL

EDITED AND WITH AN INTRODUCTION
BY HAROLD BLOOM

Printed and bound in the United States of America.

First Printing
1 3 5 7 9 8 6 4 2

Library of Congress Cataloging-in-Publication Data
applied for

ISBN 0-7910-6358-5


Chelsea House Publishers
1974 Sproul Road, Suite 400
Broomall, PA 19008-0914

The Chelsea House World Wide Web address is
http://www.chelseahouse.com

Series Editor: Matt Uhler

Contributing Editor: Janyce Marson

Produced by Publisher's Services, Santa Barbara, California

# Contents

User's Guide 7

Editor's Note 8

Introduction 10

Biography of Aristophanes 13

Introduction to Old Comedy 17

Critical Views on Greek Comedy

    Eleanor Dickey on Greek Forms of Address 21

    William E. Gruber on the Comic Hero 25

    George M. A. Grube on Literary Aspects 26

    Charles Platter on the Carnivalesque 27

    Eugene M. Waith on English Response to Aristophanes 29

Plot Summary of *The Birds* 33

List of Characters in *The Birds* 37

Critical Views on *The Birds*

    William Arrowsmith on the Symbolism of Birds 39

    Nan Dunbar on Analogue of Animal Behavior 41

    Thomas Gelzer on the Phantastic Elements 43

    Stephen Halliwell on Dual Themes of Politics and Myth 45

    Gilbert Murray on the Status of Birds 47

    Erich Segal on *The Birds* 48

Plot Summary of *The Clouds* 51

List of Characters in *The Clouds* 57

Critical Views on *The Clouds*

    William Arrowsmith on Literary Aspects 58

    Kenneth James Dover on Strepsiades' Name 60

    Rosemary M. Harriott on the Strange Ending 62

    Marie C. Marianetti on Political Satire 63

    Daphne Elizabeth O'Regan on the Nature of Justice 65

    Stella P. Revard on Percy Bysshe Shelley's Poem 67

    Ian C. Storey on Attitudes Towards the Sophists 69

Plot Summary of *The Frogs* 71

List of Characters in *The Frogs* 76

Critical Views on *The Frogs*

    Peter Arnott on the Play as Metacriticism    77

    David Barrett on Some Staging Details    79

    Maurice Croiset on the Importance of Aeschylus    80

    Joseph A. Dane on the Literary Function of Euripides    82

    Thomas K. Hubbard on *The Frogs* in Greek Literature    84

    Ismene Lada-Richards on the Cult of Dionysus    86

Plot Summary of *Lysistrata*    89

List of Characters in *Lysistrata*    93

Critical Views on *Lysistrata*

    A. M. Bowie on Treatment of Women    95

    Jeffrey Henderson on the Prologue    97

    Hans-Joachim Newiger on the Conditions in Athens    98

    Danny L. Smith on the Tragic Political Background    100

    Alan H. Sommerstein on the Turbulence in Athens    102

    Lauren K. Taaffe on Feminine Solidarity    104

    Cedric H. Whitman on Lysistrata's Feminine Nature    106

Works by Aristophanes    109

Works About Aristophanes    110

Index of Themes and Ideas    114

# User's Guide

This volume is designed to present biographical, critical, and bibliographical information on the author's best-known or most important works. Following Harold Bloom's editor's note and introduction is a detailed biography of the author, discussing major life events and important literary accomplishments. A plot summary of each play follows, tracing significant themes, patterns, and motifs in the work.

A selection of critical extracts, derived from previously published material from leading critics, analyzes aspects of each play. The extracts consist of statements from the author, if available, early reviews of the work, and later evaluations up to the present. A bibliography of the author's writings (including a complete list of all works written, cowritten, edited, and translated), a list of additional books and articles on the author and his or her work, and an index of themes and ideas in the author's writings conclude the volume.

~

**Harold Bloom** is Sterling Professor of the Humanities at Yale University and Henry W. and Albert A. Berg Professor of English at the New York University Graduate School. He is the author of over 20 books, including *Shelley's Mythmaking* (1959), *The Visionary Company* (1961), *Blake's Apocalypse* (1963), *Yeats* (1970), *A Map of Misreading* (1975), *Kabbalah and Criticism* (1975), *Agon: Toward a Theory of Revisionism* (1982), *The American Religion* (1992), *The Western Canon* (1994), and *Omens of Millennium: The Gnosis of Angels, Dreams, and Resurrection* (1996). *The Anxiety of Influence* (1973) sets forth Professor Bloom's provocative theory of the literary relationships between the great writers and their predecessors. His most recent books include *Shakespeare: The Invention of the Human,* a 1998 National Book Award finalist, and *How to Read and Why,* which was published in 2000.

Professor Bloom earned his Ph.D. from Yale University in 1955 and has served on the Yale faculty since then. He is a 1985 MacArthur Foundation Award recipient, served as the Charles Eliot Norton Professor of Poetry at Harvard University in 1987–88, and has received honorary degrees from the universities of Rome and Bologna. In 1999, Professor Bloom received the prestigious American Academy of Arts and Letters Gold Medal for Criticism.

Currently, Harold Bloom is the editor of numerous Chelsea House volumes of literary criticism, including the series BLOOM'S NOTES, BLOOM'S MAJOR DRAMATISTS, BLOOM'S MAJOR NOVELISTS, MAJOR LITERARY CHARACTERS, MODERN CRITICAL VIEWS, MODERN CRITICAL INTERPRETATIONS, and WOMEN WRITERS OF ENGLISH AND THEIR WORKS.

# Editor's Note

My introduction is an appreciation of *The Birds,* finding in it a plausible version of Cloud-Cuckooland 2002, where all of us live.

The Critical Views begin with useful remarks upon Old Comedy, with Eleanor Dickey noting conversational language as essential, and William E. Gruber considers the differences between comedy and tragedy. After which, George M. A. Grube states the preference of Aristophanes for literary rather than moral judgement; Charles Platter looks at Aristophanes through Bakhtin's spectacles; and Eugene M. Waith traces Ben Jonson's revulsion from the "bestial" Aristophanes.

The superb translator, William Arrowsmith, judges the irony of *The Birds* to be a loving one, in regard to Athenian traits, while Nan Dunbar also declines to see the play as an escape from harsh Athenian realities. Thomas Gelzer emphasizes Aristophanes' mastery of fantasy, after which Stephen Halliwell praises the play's transformations of politics into myth. For Gilbert Murray, escapism is central to *The Birds,* while the lively Erich Segal discovers in the play the true birth of comedy.

William Arrowsmith returns with an appreciation of *The Clouds* as intellectual satire, not so much of Socrates as of the Pre-Socratics. The absurd pathos of Strepsiades is recounted by Kenneth James Dover, after which Rosemary M. Harriott discuses the play's uncharacteristic negative ending. The Cloud-Chorus are seen as objects of political satire by Marie C. Marianetti, while Daphne Elizabeth O'Regan excludes moral justice from the play's cosmos. Shelley's lyric, "The Cloud," is demonstrated by Stella P. Revard to be influenced by Aristophanes's Cloud-Chorus, after which Ian C. Storey shows how subtle Aristophanes is in regard to his satirized sophist.

*The Frogs* finds Peter Arnott centering upon Dionysus as the satirized god of tragedy, while David Barrett helps us visualize the play's staging. Aristophanes' fierce preference for Aeschylus over Euripides is adumbrated by Maurice Croiset, after which Joseph A. Dane sees the play's portrait of Euripides as an authentic, originary act of literary criticism. *The Frogs* is judged to be the close of Athens's greatness by Thomas K. Hubbard, while Ismene

Lada-Richards returns us to the surprisingly comic Dionysus of Aristophanes' irreverent invention.

*Lysistrata* is seen as a dialectic of ambivalences toward women by A. M. Bowie, while Jeffrey Henderson commends Aristophanes for his skill in representing women. The play's political background is sketched by Hans-Joachim Newiger, after which Danny L. Smith gives an even darker view of Athens's tragic situation, and Alan H. Sommerstein also gives a vivid picture of that turbulence. Lauren K. Taaffe emphasizes the play's reversal of the audience's gender-expectations, after which the distinguished scholar Cedric H. Whitman sees Lysistrata as an exemplary instance of the feminine.

# Introduction

## HAROLD BLOOM

"There is a God, and his name is Aristophanes"
—Heinrich Heine

Of the eleven extant comedies of Aristophanes, the *Birds* seems best
of all to me, perhaps because it is even more outrageous than the
*Clouds* and the *Frogs*. Aristophanes, outraged by his Athens and his
Hellas, turned outrageousness into all but the highest art, to be sur-
passed only by the greatest of the Shakespearean comedies. Fortu-
nately, we have a superb version of the *Birds* by the late William
Arrowsmith, which is the text I will rely upon here.

Arrowsmith avoids the deep pit into which so many of the transla-
tors of Aristophanes have tumbled, which is to make the *Birds* or the
*Clouds* ring forth like Gilbert and Sullivan. Though imperial Athens
in 414 B.C.E. had its parallels with Victorian Britain, W. S. Gilbert's
England was not treading near disaster. In 415–414, Athens was,
when Alcibiades and his Athenian fleet sailed off to the Sicilian catastrophe. Athens was a place of hysteria, political frenzy, McCarthyite
witch-hunting, and balked aggressivity. Aristophanes therefore sends
forth his two confidence men, the daemonic Pisthetairos (let us call
him "Plausible," which his name means) and his accomplice
Euelpides ("Hopeful") to the wilderness of the Birds. There they
suborn Hoopoe, who helps persuade all the other Birds to join in the
Plausible-Hopeful project of building a New City, Cloudcuckooland.
This City of the Birds will usurp the air-space between Olympus and
Athens and so will come to dominate both. At the play's end, Plausible (who should have been played by the late Zero Mostel) is
crowned King of the cosmos, displacing Zeus, and marries Miss Uni-
verse. The wedding feast is a delicious stew of jailbirds, victims of the
Athenian-style "democracy" of King Plausible.

Any summary of outrageousness necessarily fails, particularly
because Aristophanes, in an antithetical reaction to Athenian disaster, is in hilarious high spirits throughout the *Birds*. Moses Hadas
usefully remarks that Aristophanes "erases the world that is and con-
structs another," which is in part what Heine meant when he pro-

claimed: "There is a God and his name is Aristophanes." As befits God, Aristophanes in the *Birds* avoids bitterness, happy to escape with us to Cloudcuckooland.

Prometheus, being a Titan and so anti-Olympian, arrives to offer pragmatic counsel to Plausible:

PROMETHEUS

But give me your attention. At present these Triballoi gods
have joined with Zeus to send an official embassy
to sue for peace. Now here's the policy you must follow:
flatly reject any offers of peace they make you
until Zeus agrees to restore his sceptre to the Birds
and consents to give you Miss Universe as your wife.

PISTHETAIROS

But who's Miss Universe?

PROMETHEUS

A sort of Beauty Queen,
the sign of Empire and the symbol of divine supremacy.
It's she who keeps the keys to Zeus' thunderbolts
and all his other treasures—Divine Wisdom,
Good Government, Common Sense, Naval Bases,
Slander, Libel, Political Graft, Sops to the Voters—

PISTHETAIROS

And *she* keeps the keys?

PROMETHEUS

Take it from me, friend.
Marry Miss Universe and the world is yours.
—You understand
why I had to tell you this? As Prometheus, after all,
my philanthropy is proverbial.

PISTHETAIROS

Yes, we worship you
as the inventor of the barbecue.

PROMETHEUS

Besides, I loathe the gods.

PISTHETAIROS

The loathing's mutual, I know.

PROMETHEUS

                    Just call me Timon:
I'm a misanthrope of gods.
                    —But I must be running along.
Give me my parasol. If Zeus spots me now,
he'll think I'm an ordinary one-god procession. I'll pretend
to be the girl behind the boy behind the basket.

PISTHETAIROS

Here—take this stool and watch yourself march by.

> *Exit Prometheus in solemn procession, draped in his blanket,
> the umbrella in one hand, the stool in the other. Pisthetairos
> and the Attendants retire.*

This is the *Birds* in miniature, wonderfully relevant to the United States of 2001, where Plausible II rules as our court-selected President. The sop to the Voters is of course the six-hundred-dollar-tax-rebate, even though the equivalents of Miss Universe tempted our previous ruler. Aristophanes is at his most amiable when he ends with the apotheosis of Plausible. We live in Cloudcuckooland, and why should we not? ❀

# Biography of
# Aristophanes

Aristophanes is the master poet of the old Attic comedy. While his precise date of birth is not known, scholars have relied on information from commentary within plays to place his birth approximately in the mid 5th century. Since he considered himself too young in 427 B.C. to produce a play himself, he is unlikely to have been born earlier than 460 and may have been born as late as 450 B.C. Very little is known of the playwright as ancient scholars were in a similar predicament regarding the lack of biographical information. There are sculptured portraits representing him, but they are largely unreliable as, for example, a rendition which shows Aristophanes to be an elderly man with a full crop of hair when in fact the poet was bald at an early age. Plato's *Symposium* gives us an account of a drinking party at which Aristophanes was in attendance and actually made a speech. But the details are once again highly suspect as Plato describes an event which took place in 416 (when Plato was merely eleven years old) and, therefore, this depiction is largely a product of Plato's imagination. Nevertheless, what can be adduced in the *Symposium* is that Aristophanes is well-liked and considered congenial company. At this gathering, the guests take turns making speeches in favor of Eros, or physical love. Aristophanes' speech is of great interest defining love as "the desire and pursuit of the whole." At the same time, however, Aristophanes is reported to have given a fantastical notion of the origin of sexual attraction and it is not at all clear whether he is serious or giving a brilliant and subtle parody such as that contained in *The Frogs*.

Aristophanes was born into a radical democracy created and strengthened by his father, Philippus, and grandfather. He grew up at a time in which Athens was near the peak of its power and authority in the Greek world, during an era of political and cultural life dominated by Perikles. Some notable events during the 440s and 430s were the building of the Parthenon, a monument to the imperial leadership and wealth of Athens, and the rise of the city as the center of artistic and intellectual life, and the focal point for trade and tourism which brought Athens into contact with the entire Mediterranean and beyond. At this time, Athens was at the head of an alliance of Greek cities which alliance gradually lead to into an empire and, towards the end of this time, brought it into confrontation with Sparta. That conflict lead to the outbreak of hostilities in 431 and ended with the defeat of Athens in 404. Thus, the bulk of Aristophanes' career took place at a time in which Athens's hegemony was being challenged, while the latter part of his career witnessed the rebuilding of the city and the emergence of a new leadership. The spirit of his work reflects both the former predominance and later reestablishment of Athens. One the one hand, his work is an expression of freedom and exuberance, of democratic and cultural self confidence during a time of prosperity between 470 and 430 B.C. On the other hand, his work also reflects a time in which Athens' self-confidence is being tested and threatened with an enormous conflict. War indeed becomes the inaugural event in *Lysistrata*.

It has been inferred (wrongly, perhaps) from Archanians that he lived, or owned property, on Aegina, an island in the Saronic Gulf. Aegina was of literary importance in the early 5th century for the odes written by Pindar, a lyric poet commissioned to write poems for state functions commemorating athletic achievements and victories. The ode held a very prominent political and religious status in ancient Greece. It was a very formal poem suited to praising the city and honoring the god of the games; it also reminded the victor of his moral duties and offered prayers meant to avert misfortune.

In the first period, down to 421, Aristophanes wrote a comedy for each of the major festivals for which he won many first prizes, thus establishing himself, along with his close contemporary, Eupolis, as an outstanding playwright of his generation. Aristophanes' distinction was to satirize Cleon, a prominent politician and the strongest leader since the death of Pericles. After 421, Aristophanes makes a shift away from satirizing a particular politician and directs his energies to the pursuit of comic originality. *The Clouds* provides some evidence for this shift where Aristophanes mocks his rivals' interests. From *The Birds* (414 B.C.) onwards, Aristophanes added some new features such as the introduction of choral songs irrelevant to the subject matter of the play and, in *Plutus* (408 B.C.), the chorus becomes somewhat of an impediment to the unfolding of the plot. All of this suggests that Aristophanes had earned a literary preeminence which entitled him to improvise and redefine the conventional rules of the comedy.

As demonstrated in each of the four plays discussed below, Aristophanes has a brilliant imagination combined with colorful language and a very keen perception of and appreciation for the absurd, whether the spectacle of two old and disenchanted Athenians in *The Birds* advocating the foundation of a new city which would overthrow the traditional Olympian gods, the ludicrous characterization of the god Dionysus in *The Frogs;* the imposition of a temporary government of women in *Lysistrata;* or the characterization of Socrates' victim, Pheidippides, in *The Clouds,* as both foolish and dishonest, given to displays of bad temper and sexual obsession. Using the modes of satire, parody and fantastical exaggeration, his plays are unforgettable in their multifaceted critique of politics, the poets, the scientists, the philosophers and professors of rhetoric and persuasive argumentation. On the other side of the spectrum, his sympathetic characters are citizens who want to enjoy their lives without governmental interference, while advocating ingenious schemes, sometimes to the point of taking violent action in the service of achieving what they consider to be their inalienable right to happiness. However, sympathetic or otherwise, no class or profession is wholly exempt from criticism.

In the final analysis, because of the scope of his subject matter, Aristophanes becomes the chronicler of social change of his time. He has likewise credited for having elevated the intellectual and artistic standards of comedy. Nevertheless, his political and moral influence cannot claim the same level of achievement. Most notably, both Plato and Xenophon blame Aristophanes' portrayal of Socrates in *The Clouds* for having caused the mistrust, and eventual execution, of Socrates. In that play, Aristophanes depicts the philosopher as one willing to teach his students "how to make the weaker argument the stronger," an accusation frequently brought against the sophists. Socrates was accused of impiety in having introduced new gods and corrupting young men. While these charges may very well have been nothing more than an excuse used by his political opponents, Socrates was put to death by drinking hemlock on 399 B.C. In response to his tragic death, Plato and Xenophon wrote rebuttals against the charges brought against Socrates, rebuttals in which he is shown to have refused payment for his teaching. While Xenophon portrays Socrates as holding traditional values concerning virtue, Plato emphasizes the fact that he never presented himself as a teacher of any subject, unlike the other sophists.

Aristophanes died in or shortly before 386. Eleven of his plays survive; and, in addition, there are 32 titles (some of them alternative titles, and some certainly attributed to other authors) and nearly a thousand fragments and citations. While his plays have aroused curiosity for later writers, their influence has not been too great due to both problems of translation and difficulty in comprehending his ethical issues, most notably problems with the scurrility of his satire, the irreverent treatment of religious matters and an unparalleled degree of obscenity in comparison with other ancient literary works. Nevertheless, it is these very same features that make Aristophanes so unique in the ancient world. ❀

# Introduction to Old Comedy

Classical scholars have categorized Ancient Greek comedy into three chronological divisions: Old, Middle, and New. The features of Old Comedy, in which Aristophanes' work remains the best example, are a mixture of dance, poetry, song and drama, combining fantastic plots and sharp satire of contemporary events and people. It is important to recognize that this earliest category of comedy is associated with democracy and freedom of speech. Middle Comedy, which flourished from approximately 400 to 388 B.C., is mainly associated with Aristophanes' last surviving play, *Plutus* (388 B.C.) and is much milder in its criticism, satirizing types of people rather than individuals, and speaking in very general terms of the evils of society rather than discussing specific corruption and political problems. Middle Comedy takes place in an environment in which freedom of speech is repressed following the defeat of Athens in the Peloponnesian War. New Comedy began to appear around 336 B.C. and it features a chorus which has been transformed into a group of singers and dancers performing in interludes rather than participating in a significant part in the play. Here, the characters and situations are drawn from contemporary life and the plots are chiefly designed around domestic problems and conflicts, such as love, marriage and offspring, and the characters are principally types rather than individuals. Though many comedies were written in this style, only one entire play by Menander survives.

A common feature in many preliterate cultures was the public occasion in which its people would pretend humorously to assume someone else's identity and, with this characteristic in mind, it is very possible that comedy may in fact be of earlier antiquity than the tragedy. The primitive *komos* or ritual revelry, in which an often inebriated procession took place accompanied by song and dance, is considered to be an early stage in the development of Old Comedy. In the 4th century B.C. it appears that a humorous adult chorus was an archaic feature at the City Dionysia and that comedy evolved from this type of chorus. The City Dionysia belonged to the cult of Dionysus from the village of Eleutherae ("of the black goatskin") which believed that Dionysus had driven the daughters of Eleuther to madness. This festival, held during March and April when the city was filled with visitors, would begin with a procession bearing the image of Dionysus to the theatre (located at the south slope of the Acropolis), and then proceed along an unknown route, carrying phalli, loaves and bowls, to the sacred precinct where animals were sacrificed and bloodless offerings were made. Both tragedians and comic poets competed at these festivals. The other Dionysiac festival was celebrated in Athens in January and February, and its name is a derived from the word "maenad," referring to the women who were driven to ritual frenzy by Dionysus. There was a procession and a mystic ritual and much of what is known is from the rituals depicted on the "Lenaea vases." At the Lenaea, the contests in comedy were similar to that of the City Dionysia, but here, the comic poets had greater significance than the tragedians. Despite the artistic elevation of Old Comedy, with increasingly higher standards of poetry, drama and theatre, the underlying comic impulse is derived from the carnivalesque absurdity and vulgarity of its folk origins.

There are three sources of evidence which confirm existence of a comedic chorus: (1) an Attic black figure amphora of the mid-6th century which portrays a group of men disguised as horses, with riders on their back, accompanied by a flute-player and thus is an early example of the animal chorus in Aristophanes and other playwrights of the 5th century; (2) 6th century vase paintings (including those of Attica) portraying either dancers in exaggerated dress for humorous effect, at times wearing a phallus of exaggerated size, or a variety of satyrs in either phallic or grotesque costume; and (3) poems of the 7th century, by Archilochus and at the end of the 6th century (by Hipponax) which contain unrestrained satire and gross sexual humor.

As for the more conjectural, but highly probable source, Aristotle's *Poetics* contains the earliest and best-known theory regarding the origins of ancient Greek comedy. Aristotle's analysis begins on the basis that the origins of tragedy and comedy were to be sought in the festivals of Dionysus which were widespread throughout the Greek world and the ribald, sexual content which he saw as a derivative of the earlier "genre" of phallic song. Furthermore, there is a connection between sexuality and fertility that occurs frequently in Old Comedy that seems to suggest such beginnings in improvised phallic processions. As Aristotle points out, however, the early history of comedy as a dramatic form is unknown. A significant issue regarding origins is raised by K. J. Dover, who says that "one element in Aristophanes which does seem to be old and to have no discernible connection with phallic songs is the animal disguises of the chorus." (*Aristophanic Comedy,* University of California Press, 1972 p. 219). It seems likely that the two traditions—the phallic and animal choruses—along with others emerging from Athens and Sicily, were already incorporated as they were adapted in its later development. At Athens comedies were presented at the festivals in honor of Dionysus, the Great Dionysia and the Lenaea (during January and February).

The structure of Old Comedy has at least some, if not all, of the following elements: (1) a *kommation* or prologue, which explains the essential elements of the plot; (2) a *parodos,* the entrance song and dance of the chorus; (3) an *agon,* a contest or dispute, which is the essential conflict of the play; (4) a *parabasis* ("coming forward"), an address to the audience by the chorus during intermission in the action, alone and speaking for the author without their masks, which consists of an *anapest,* a passage in which the chorus often discusses a political or literary subject; (b) a *pnigos* ("choker," to be recited in one breath), one long sentence recited at a high pitch of excitement in one breath; (c) an ode addressed to a god; (d) an *epirrhema* ("that said afterwards"), a speech on contemporary matters, its contents were satire, advice or exhortation; (e) an antode ("opposite song"), similar to the ode, contained an invocation to the gods or muse to assist the chorus, and finally (f) an *antistrophe* ("counterturning"), which returns to the comic mood; (5) several episodes separated by choral odes; and (6) the *exodos,* the conclusion, in which all rejoice in a revel (*komos*) or a marriage (*gamos*) or both.

From the evidence of Aristophanes' plays the plots of Old Comedy were fantastic and the characters essentially caricatures. The characters wore everyday clothing and highly stylized masks. The twenty-four members of the chorus were sometimes divided into two groups. Only brief fragments remains of the works of the writers of Old Comedy who were contemporaries and rivals of Aristophanes: Cratinus (c. 520-423 B.C.), whom Aristophanes ridicules in *The Knights,* and Eupolis (c. 446–411 B.C.). Thus, the plays of Aristophanes are the sole surviving examples of this brilliant form. His fantastic plots and his extravagant, grotesque, and licentious wit demonstrate that he is both a consummate playwright of the truly comic while, simultaneously addressing the profoundly serious aspects of the political, social and literary conflicts of his time.

As Stephen Halliwell points out with respect to stage directions, there is very little literary evidence as to details. Beyond the seating of the audience, there was a substantial, probably wooden, stage building and, in front of it, a larger performance area known as the *orchestra* (literally, dancing floor), with an entrance/exit on either side, used by both actors and chorus. Aristophanes also made use of a *méchané* (machine), a type of crane which suspended characters in simulated flight. Most of the comedies were performed by three main actors and all roles were played by males, who wore body stockings with appropriate anatomical details, when playing the role of women. Masks were also worn and they were typically very exaggerated as were the characterizations in the play. The chorus consisted of twenty-four singers/dancers with musical accompaniment provided by a piper.

Finally, it should also be remembered that Aristophanes' work is a public art form which seeks not so much to lecture as to cause the audience to look at itself. While we come to expect modern day satire as poking fun at an individual public figure, Aristophanes often makes fun of his audience and, at other times, he presents an unfavorable perspective of the city and its behavior. In a word, Aristophanes holds up a mirror to his audience which not only reflects back, but also distorts the picture in order to emphasize its problems. In the end, the satire and fantastical situations in the plays move the audience well beyond amusement to a more serious consideration of their own civic responsibilities. ✿

# Critical Views on
## Greek Comedy

ELEANOR DICKEY ON GREEK FORMS OF ADDRESS

[Eleanor Dickey is the author of *Greek Forms of Address: From Herodotus to Lucian* (1996). In the excerpt below from her article, "Forms of Address and Conversational Language," Dickey discusses the relationship between comic and conversational language in Arisophanes. ]

The problem of the relationship of comic language to conversational Attic has been increasingly discussed in recent years, although at an earlier period it was sometimes taken for granted that the language of comedy must be identical to that of colloquial spoken Greek. The question of comic language is of course a large and complex one, and at the present time it would be extremely difficult to examine all its aspects in a systematic way. The smaller and more quantifiable area of vocative usage, however, can provide some valuable evidence about the type of language used by Aristophanes and Menander.

The first question for a study of this type is exactly what standard to use for the evaluation of comic language, and this decision will have important consequences. We are not seeking 'spoken Greek', a nebulous concept taking no account of different registers and genres of speech, but rather conversational Attic. ⟨. . .⟩

How then might conversational Attic be related to the genres we possess, tragedy, comedy, and prose? The traditional wisdom is that tragedy represents the most elevated type of language and the one most remote from ordinary speech, comedy the lowest level and that closest to daily conversation, and prose a level somewhere in between. If a distinction is made between Aristophanes and Menander, it is that Menander's language is more elevated that of Aristophanes and thus further from the conversational genre. These assumptions make possible studies of colloquialisms in tragedy and prose by comparison with comedy, since comic language is taken to be virtually identical to conversational Attic.

All the evidence indicates that this ordering of the genres is correct in terms of its classification of the elevation of language; that is, tragic language was certainly meant to be elegant, comic language (at least that of Aristophanes) was often meant to be vulgar, and Plato's language aimed neither at excessive elevation nor at great vulgarity. Thus far the traditional view is virtually unassailable, but what are the grounds for assuming that conversational language must be equated with the lowest of these levels? ⟨. . .⟩

Yet what is in fact the definition of conversational language? I would define conversational language as that used in casual conversations by people who were not thinking about their use of language at the time. ⟨. . .⟩ In Athens, there were probably linguistic differences between men and women, citizens and slaves, and natives and immigrants. Within the range of the conversational genre, 'low' language would have been that associated with people of lower status in the society, such as slaves, and 'high' language would have been that normally used by people of higher rank.

There is no reason why any one of these types of conversational language should be regarded as more authentic than any other; the language that an educated Athenian used in talking to his family has just as much claim to be considered 'conversational' as the language that his slaves used in talking to their families. Thus there is no reason to assume that all conversational language will be equivalent to the 'lowest' literary genre available. ⟨. . .⟩

If the writers of Greek prose and comedy were being absolutely realistic in imitating conversational language, then, we would expect to find a variety of different types of speech in their works, ranging from the language of educated citizens to that of slaves and foreigners. In fact, distinctions in language between Athenians and foreigners are prominent in Aristophanes, whose plays contain Spartans, Megarians, and Boeotians speaking conspicuously non-Attic dialects.

—Eleanor Dickey, "Forms of Address and Conversational Language," *Mnemosyne* 48, no. 3 (June 1995): pp. 258–61.

[William E. Gruber is the author of *Missing Persons: Character and Characterization in Modern Drama* (1994) and *Comic Theaters: Studies in Performance and Audience Response* (1986). In the excerpt below from his article, "The Wild Men of Comedy: Transformations in the Comic Hero from Aristophanes to Pirandello," Gruber discusses the genre of comedy in Western literature with specific reference to Aristophanes and the element of surprise. ]

My subject in this essay is the hero of Western stage comedy, in particular as he testifies to the persistence of a specific dramatic form, a continuing mode of theater. For many, I realize, the term "comic hero" remains a contradiction in terms, since we do not normally link the words comic and heroic. That it makes sense to do so is a position which I hope at least partially to justify in the course of my discussion. ⟨. . .⟩

Comedy especially seems to mock those who attempt to isolate and to define it, making a joke out of the intended definition. Viewed as humor, Comedy often dies in its own explanation; viewed as dramatic art, Comedy includes plays whose prodigious variety cannot easily be subsumed according to meaningful types. ⟨. . .⟩ Despite such reservations, however, I do not believe (as L. C. Knights did) that essays in comedy are "necessarily" barren exercises. Broadly speaking, my aim in this essay is to stimulate discussion, rather than to settle it. I hope to provide something of substance nonetheless, if only because the subject itself is endlessly fascinating. Comedy seems particularly relevant for a world in which, it has been suggested, "exuberance verges on desperation and laughter is suspect as a form of sedition." ⟨. . .⟩

A number of things follow from this. First, it will be seen that comedy tends instinctively, as it were, to move away from what we normally call "dramatic" toward the theatrical; comedy emphasizes, to borrow terms from Coleridge's lectures on Shakespeare, surprise over expectation. This is obvious enough in the dramatic cartoons of Aristophanes, but true as well of the elaborately orchestrated comedies of Shakespeare, who freights all his comedies with generous measures of the marvelous. The observation also illustrates, perversely enough, how simply Beckett can distort a comic bias to tragic ends: what, after all, could be more unanticipated—more laughable—than a play in which nothing happens? And yet what ultimately could be more frightening, to extend Henri Bergson's description of a comic situation, then to meet a friend unexpectedly in the course of a day, not three or four times, but twenty or one hundred? Here, as in Beckett's drama, the laughable segues into the frightening, the comic into the tragic: for the mechanical is not merely encrusted upon the living, the mechanical is all there is. Beckett's drama returns us, ironically, to the centuries-old tragic insights: "nothing to be done."

It follows as well that tragedy and comedy, thus parted on the central issue of irony, tend to organize themselves as formal aesthetic opposites on a single scale, oriented toward each other as well as toward the reality they have traditionally been assumed to imitate. *A Midsummer Night's Dream* and *Romeo and Juliet* make sense as formal opposites, an aesthetic judgment which, incidentally, can be partly substantiated by evidence surrounding their composition. So, too, New Comedy has been termed "a comic Oedipus situation," and a play like Aristophanes' *The Birds* can be understood as a flippant answer to the gloom of Aeschylean tragedy: even Zeus, it seems, can be overcome. Something like this formal opposition of comedy and tragedy is described by Northrop Frye who writes that "just as comedy often sets up an arbitrary law and then organizes the action to break or evade it, so tragedy presents the reverse theme of narrowing a comparatively free life into a process of causation"—save that by "law" Frye means not causality generally but only a law which is morally suspicious or practically unenforceable, which the comedy then modifies or removes from the books altogether. The truth of the matter is that comedy abrogates particular legal or moral conventions only as a means better to annihilate probability generally. Puck, recall, prefers "those things which befall preposterously," and his comedy obediently turns everything possible hind foremost.

—William E. Gruber, "The Wild Men of Comedy: Transformations in the Comic Hero from Aristophanes to Pirandello," *Genre* 14, no. 2 (Summer 1981): pp. 207–8, 211–12.

## George M. A. Grube on Literary Aspects

[George M. A. Grube has translated *The Trial and Death of Socrates: Euthyphro, Apology, Crito, Death Scene from Phaedo / Plato* (2000) and is the author of *A Greek Critic: Demetrius on Style* (1961). In the excerpt below from the chapter entitled "Comedy: Aristophanes," Grube discusses the literary aspects of the comedies.]

In view of the important place of poetry, and of tragic drama in particular, in the social life of Athens, it was entirely natural that comedies of this nature should pay considerable attention to poetry and drama. Literary allusions, criticisms and parodies abound throughout, and Aristophanes clearly expected his audience to recognize them, to an extent quite impossible on our own comic stage. Moreover, two whole comedies have literary subjects: the *Thesmaphoriazusae* which satirizes Euripides, and the *Frogs* with its contest between Aeschylus and Euripides for the Chair of Tragedy in Hades; there are also several literary scenes in the other plays. We do not, of course, expect impartial judgements from Aristophanes, but his criticisms are often acute and he incidentally formulates a number of critical principles which we meet here for the first time.

He was also the first, as far as we know, to give clear expression to the old Greek feeling that poets are teachers. As Aeschylus puts it in the *Frogs* (1054–5): 'Children are taught at school, but poets are the teachers of men', and Aristophanes willingly accepted this responsibility for himself. He does not hesitate to criticize the policies or leaders of the nation. ⟨. . .⟩

The famous attack on Socrates in the *Clouds* is mainly an attack on the rhetorical education of the sophists, with which the real Socrates had nothing to do, but Aristophanes brings in philosophy, the new poetry, Euripides, the new music and cheerfully lumps them all together. So Strepsiades has to submit to grammatical studies and worship the new philosophical gods. Then the great debate between the right and the wrong *Logoi* is full of Euripidean echoes. The quarrel between Strepsiades and his son started when the boy, being more modernly educated, wants to quote from Euripides instead of from old Simonides or Aeschylus. He then argues from animal life in the manner of the younger sophists, to justify the most outrageous conduct.

We need not endorse Aristophanes' condemnation of it all, but he was to a large degree justified in linking together these different aspects of the new thought, for they all challenged tradition, whether social, political, religious, educational, musical or literary. And he was certainly right to see in Euripides the representative of the new scepticism on the tragic stage. ⟨. . .⟩

Shortly after the death of Euripides, Aristophanes produced the *Frogs*. It is the most important critical document we possess from the fifth century, and probably the most amusing in the whole history of criticism. Dionysus, the god of tragedy, visits Heracles, who, as an old traveller to the underworld, may be able to give him useful hints; he explains that he has been reading the *Andromeda* and has decided to go down to Hades to fetch Euripides back, for he was a skilful poet ⟨. . .⟩. Heracles asks what's wrong with those now living, and they review them briefly. What of Iophon, the son of Sophocles? Well, he's the only good thing left but we cannot be sure yet. Why not fetch back Sophocles instead of Euripides? We'll just wait and see what Iophon is like on his own; besides, Euripides is such a clever rogue, he'll find ways to help in his escape, whereas Sophocles was always such an easy-going fellow. Where's Agathon? He's left us to join the banquets of the blessed; a pity, he was a good poet and his friends miss him. Xenocles? Pythangelus?

HERACLES:  Aren't there other little lads writing innumerable tragedies, more loquacious than Euripides by a mile?
DIONYSUS:  Yes, tiny grapes not worth the picking, mere chatterboxes; they produce one play, befoul tragedy once, and are never heard of again. You won't find a creative poet, look where you will.
HERACLES:  How do you mean, creative?
DIONYSUS:  By creative I mean one who will venture some such bold phrase as 'Ether, halls of Zeus', or 'the foot of time', speak of a mind unwilling to take a sacred oath, the tongue having forsworn itself without the mind.
HERACLES:  You like these things?
DIONYSUS:  I'm quite crazy about them.

Heracles thinks they're all nonsense, but as Dionysus rudely reminds him, he is hardly an expert: 'You teach me to eat.'

The whole scene makes clear that Aristophanes, who had ridiculed and satirized Euripides on the stage for over twenty years, fully recognized his genius and unhesitatingly classes him with Aeschylus and Sophocles as one of the three great tragedians of Athens. That verdict has never been disputed. We should note that in this scene there is no question of any moral judgement.

—George M. A. Grube, "Comedy: Aristophanes," *The Greek and Roman Critics* (Canada: University of Toronto Press and Great Britain: Robert Cunningham and Sons Ltd., 1965): pp. 22–26.

## CHARLES PLATTER ON THE CARNIVALESQUE

[Charles Platter is an editor of *Sex and Gender in Medieval and Renaissance Texts: The Latin Tradition* (1997) and an editor of *Rethinking Sexuality: Foucault and Classical Antiquity* (1998). In the excerpt below from his article entitled "The Uninvited Guest: Aristophanes in Bakhtin's 'History of Laughter,'" Platter discusses Bakhtin's definition of the carnivalesque as a parody of the social order.]

This essay has two basic intentions: first to discuss Bakhtin's idea of carnival culture as he formulates it in the case of Rabelais and to consider its possible application to Athenian Old Comedy, particularly to Aristophanes; secondly, to reformulate Bakhtin's account of the carnival in such a way as to join it to dialogue, a key term in the Bakhtinian lexicon. It is within this context, I suggest, that the idea of the carnivalesque can be meaningfully applied to Aristophanes and can begin to contribute to a political interpretation of the rich profusion of speech genres and styles that comprise Aristophanic comedy. Among the most difficult of these genres and, potentially, the most rewarding is the phenomenon of tragic parody, the implicit challenge issued by Aristophanes in the name of comedy to tragedy and any discourse that presents itself as self–sufficient and complete or, to use Bakhtin's term, "finalized." ⟨. . .⟩

Since carnival in Bakhtin's sense expresses itself by degrading the prevailing hierarchies and institutions, its dominant forms of expression are parodic: "We find here a characteristic logic, the peculiar logic of the 'inside out,' of the 'turnabout,' of a continual shifting from top to bottom, from front to rear, of numerous parodies, travesties, profanations, comic crownings and uncrownings." ⟨. . .⟩

Readers of Aristophanes have understandably seized upon the above features as characteristic of Aristophanic comedy as well and have sought to extend the application of Bakhtin's model in that direction. Such features of Aristophanic comedy as its unrestrained obscenity, its self–conscious mixture of styles, tragic parody, relentless obsession with food and the presence of ⟨*spoudogeloion*⟩, the quality that for Bakhtin gives laughter its philosophical, liberating aspect, all have distinct parallels in the "carnivalistic" mode of discourse Bakhtin attributes to Medieval/Renaissance folk culture and, by extension, to Rabelais. Bakhtin himself admits as much in his essay "Forms of Time and Chronotope in the Novel":

> The direct influence of Aristophanes on the works of Rabelais is evidence of a deep internal kinship (again via pre–class folklore). Here again we find on a different level of development the same reworking of everything that is private and everyday, the same heroics of the comic and the absurd, the same sexual indecencies, the same matrices of food and drink.

Recent studies about comedy such as those of Rosen, Carrière and Rösler assume this parallel, and for some very good reasons. There exists, therefore, a strong prima facie case for the inclusion of Aristophanes within Bakhtin's tradition of carnival laughter. At the same time Aristophanes is conspicuously absent from Bakhtin's account of the precursors of Rabelais and from his "prehistory of the novel." In a recent article, José Suárez has argued that this omission is unintentional. Suárez quite correctly regards Aristophanic comedy as an authentic serio–comic genre. He quotes *Problems of Dostoevsky's Poetics* for Bakhtin's list of external characteristics for literature that is genuinely serio–comic and carnivalistic: (a) that the starting point for the understanding of the dramatic situation is the present; (b) that the plots are not based on legend, but on experience and are frequently critical of the society they represent; (c) that serio–comic genres reject the stylistic unity of epic and tragedy, instead mixing styles and tones, serious and comic. Suárez proceeds to analyze the *Frogs* and has little difficulty showing that these features are present in Aristophanes. ⟨. . .⟩

Aristophanic laughter overwhelms all and thus becomes a separate world of its own, a sort of "comic myth" incapable of entering into a dialogic relationship with the world it represents. In Bakhtin's view, therefore, there is something about Aristophanic laughter that undermines its self–conscious claim to seriousness. He goes on to refer to "individualized and typically everyday features in Aristophanes—whose living wholeness has been annihilated by laughter." One might imagine he has in mind passages such as the *agon* of the *Clouds,* where the victory of the Unjust Speech is brought about by the powerful claim that absolutely everyone from politicians and orators to tragedians and spectators is drawn from the contemptible ranks of the pathic ⟨*euryproctoi*⟩ (1083–1100). Here the Old Comedy tradition of personal invective ⟨. . .⟩ and the frequent claim of the comic poet to advise the city and identify its enemies collapses with his indulgence in a leveling ridicule that lumps together everyone and consequently cannot distinguish a Cratinus from a Cleon.

—Charles Platter, "The Uninvited Guest: Aristophanes in Bakhtin's 'History of Laughter,'" *Arethusa* 26, no. 2 (Spring 1993): pp. 201–5.

## EUGENE M. WAITH ON ENGLISH RESPONSE TO ARISTOPHANES

[Eugene M. Waith is the author of *Patterns and Perspectives in English Renaissance Drama* (1988) and an editor of *Titus Andronicus* (1984). In the excerpt below from his article entitled "Aristophanes, Plautus, Terence, and the Refinement of English Comedy," Waith discusses some seventeenth and eighteenth century reactions to Aristophanes.]

⟨. . .⟩ The very history of comedy from its origins in Greece to its Roman manifestations in Plautus and Terence—the standard account of the development of classical comedy—may have a considerable bearing on the refinement of English comedy. ⟨. . .⟩

⟨. . .⟩ Among these was *Eupolis, Cratinus,* and *Aristophanes;* but afterward the order of thys wryting Comedies was reformed and made more plausible: then wrytte *Plato* (*Comicus*), *Menander,* and I knowe not who more." ⟨. . .⟩ Aristophanes' notorious satire of Sophocles in *The Clouds* is often held up as a horrible example of the excesses of Old Comedy. Ben Jonson, one of those who refers to the treatment of Sophocles, adds a few other details which recur with increasing frequency in later characterizations of Old Comedy. The passage from *Discoveries* in which they appear is largely taken from the Dutch scholar Heinsius:

> . . . it was cleare that all insolent, and obscene speaches; jest[s] upon the best men; injuries to particular persons; perverse, and sinister Sayings (and the rather unexpected) in the old Comedy, did move laughter; especially, where it did imitate any dishonesty; and scurrility came forth in the place of wit: which who understands the nature and *Genius* of laughter, cannot but perfectly know.
>
> Of which *Aristophanes* affords an ample harvest, having not only outgone *Plautus,* or any other in that kinde; but express'd all the moods, and figures, of what is ridiculous, oddly. In short, as Vinegar is not accounted good, untill the wine be corrupted: so jests that are true and naturall, seldome raise laughter, with the beast, the multitude. They love nothing, that is right, and proper. The farther it runs from reason, or possibility with them, the better it is. What could have made them laugh, like to see *Socrates* presented, that Example of all good life, honesty, and vertue, to have him hoisted up with a Pullie, and there play the philosopher, in a basquet? . . . This is truly leaping from the Stage to the Trumbrell againe, reducing all witt to the originall Dungcart.

Here not only the bitter personal satire but the scurrility and absurdity are regrettable, worthy only of the laughter of a bestial multitude.

Jonson probably knew that for similar reasons Plutarch preferred Menander to Aristophanes: "Coarseness . . . in words, vulgarity and ribaldry are present in Aristophanes, but not at all in Menander; obviously, for the uneducated, ordinary person is captivated by what the former says, but the educated man will be displeased." The educated man was pleased, on the other hand, by what he took to be the regularity of New Comedy, arranged in acts according to schemes explained by the fourth-century commentators. ⟨. . .⟩

The learned Anne Dacier, to whose translation and commentary Echard is indebted, says that while some of the "plaisanteries" and "railleries" in Plautus are fine and delicate, others are tasteless and gross, whereas all of them in Terence are graces which do not cause laughter but give a pleasure no less keen. Terence, then, is free of a certain coarseness which occasionally disfigures Plautus, as if in the growth of Roman comedy there were a phylogenetic repetition of the evolution of New Comedy. Several critics comment on the parallels. In the preface to his translation of Plautus Echard, recalling Caesar's term for Terence, says: ". . . as the later was call'd the *Half Menander,* so the former may be stil'd the *Half Aristophanes.*"

The standard treatment of the history of classical comedy provides an analogue to the procedure described by George Kubler in *The Shape of Time,* where he speaks of the use by historians of art of biological metaphors such as birth, death, flowering, maturity, and fading. "However useful it is for pedagogical purposes," he writes, "the biological metaphor of style as a sequence of life-stages was historically misleading, for it bestowed upon the flux of events the shapes and the behavior of organisms." The endlessly repeated story of which I have given a few examples makes it seem that comedy, having profited by the discipline which its childish waywardness brought upon it, achieved maturity in Menander and again in Terence. ⟨. . .⟩

Given the common assumption that the life of the mind is superior to the life of sensation, formulation of the distinctions between Old and New Comedy and between Plautus and Terence in terms of grossness and refinement inevitably suggested a pattern of growth or progress. ⟨. . .⟩ The foundation for the progressivist history was laid by Aristotle and Horace.

One implication of such a history is that comedy from Aristophanes to Terence became more what it should be or what it essentially is. The very definitions of comedy favored this opinion. When George Whetstone writes: ". . . to worke a Comedie kindly, graue olde men should instruct, yonge men should showe the imperfections of youth, Strumpets should be lascivious, Boyes vnhappy, and Clownes should speake disorderlye," he is obviously thinking of New Comedy rather than of Aristophanes. Even Aristotle's statement that "Comedy is . . . an imitation of characters of a lower type" applies better to New Comedy. ⟨. . .⟩ Although some of the characters of

Aristophanes seem to be based on the observation of ordinary people, especially in his last surviving play, *Plutus* (for many years the most read), it was Menander who received from a Byzantine critic the ecstatic apostrophe: "Menander and Life! Which of you imitated the other?"

— Eugene M. Waith, "Aristophanes, Plautus, Terence, and the Refinement of English Comedy," *Studies in the Literary Imagination* 10, no. 1 (Spring 1977): pp. 91–95.

# Plot Summary of
## *The Birds*

A play written in the style of Old Comedy, won first prize in 414 B.C. in the City Dionysia. It is constructed around an elaborate fantasy about a clever Athenian who persuades the birds to build a city in the clouds and compels the gods to accept humiliating terms.

The opening scene takes place in a wild and desolate wilderness with Euelpides, holding a jackdaw on his wrist and Pisthetairos, holding a crow. They are also carrying their belongings, which consist of a basket, various pots, cooking skewers, myrtle wreaths and bedding, some of which suggest an anticipated sacrifice to the gods, and both of them enter while speaking to their birds. However, neither of them really knows where they are. The two old men are tired of paying taxes to Athens and of the endless litigation in which the Athenians are engaged, they "[s]it in the courts and whine throughout their lives!" and have decided to leave the city and seek a home in a more peaceful spot, "to roam in search of a land that's free of trouble." Their goal is "to find where Tereus lives, the hoopoe," for the mythological king has been metamorphosed as a hoopoe bird, in order to ask the hoopoe if, while flying about, he has observed a quiet place where they might settle down, a "city that's warm and woolly." When the two elderly men meet Tereus' bird servant, they are told that his master still retains some human characteristics, at times choosing to eat anchovies rather than a bird's diet of myrtle berries and gnats. And when the two finally meet Tereus, they are overwhelmed by his huge beak and vestigial plumage, to which Tereus responds in anger, declaring that he is still part human and, further, that their disparaging remarks are "the sort of outrage Sophokles / Inflicts on me in those tragic plays of his." However, the Hoopoe soon collects himself, asking them why they are here, and when they state that they are in search of a pleasant city that offers simple pastimes and is free of corruption and taxes (which they are determined to evade), the Hoopoe suggests various places, all of which they find objectionable because it will lead to discovery and arrest by the Athenian government. Nevertheless, as the Hoopoe listens to Euelpides and Pisthetairos plead their cause, that they are here in search of "a city that's warm and woolly—/ [a] place to curl up in, like a big soft blanket," he is impressed by their conception of founding a new city. Most importantly, however, their visioned new city, in which the birds will reign above man, is premised on a transgression of the powers granted to many of the Greek gods and, accordingly, as will be seen, these proposed violations will cause great trouble once the city is established. Nevertheless, the Hoopoe proceeds to summon an assembly of many different birds to discuss the idea with them. Not surprisingly, the birds are quite nervous that these two human beings are about to encroach upon their turf, and proclaim that "[o]ur world's betrayed, we've been defiled!" Indeed, the birds' suspicion of the two Athenians is so great that they begin to attack Euelpides and Pisthetairos. When the Hoopoe finally reestablishes peace, the two Athenians explain their utopian project and the justification for their reclaiming what originally belonged to them before the gods took over, even to the extreme point of imposing a taxation on the gods. Pisthetairos points out that the birds ruled men before the gods did; if they now build their city between earth and heaven they can force both men and gods to worship them. "If the gods don't pay the tribute you demand / This aerial city of yours won't give free passage / To the smoke of sacrifice from earth below." The Chorus gladly accepts the plan and, in the first parabasis, speaks to the audience, which, it says is unfortunately limited and mortal, "wingless creatures-of-a-day, pathetic dreamlike / humans," who are ignorant of the origin, nature, and glory of birds and of their great value to man. If the members of the audience are weary of their restricted lives as men, they may join the birds and live freely and happily. "The birds will show them where to find old buried / [h]oards of silver" and states that the birds will grant a longer life to humans for "[f]rom their reserves / [r]emember that 'five human ages lives the cawing crow.'"

Shortly thereafter, the two old Athenians who now reappear with wings attached, proceed to laugh at each other's transformation. Pisthetairos tells Euelpides that he looks like "a painted goose, and a cheap one too!" And Euelpides responds that Pisthetairos looks like "a blackbird whose / [s]calp's been cropped!" But their banter soon stops as their attention quickly turns to the need for a name for their new city. They agree on the name Cloudcuckooland for their utopian scheme. Indeed, the word utopia literally means no place and, thus, it is a mere figment of the imagination. Nevertheless, desirous of implementing their fantastical plan, Pisthetairos sends Euelpides to help build the walls and other parts of the city. Pisthetairos, with the help of a priest, prays to various bird gods and interviews a poet, a scientist, an oracle-monger, and others who wish to do work for the new city, but rejects all of them. He declares the poet to be a "nuisance," dismisses the oracle-monger as a "charlatan," "[m]eddling in other men's rites, and seeking a share of the / innards," and succeeds in intimidating Meton, the scientist and town planner about the likelihood of violent reaction amongst the bird population, and suggests that he make his great escape while he still can. "Just scarper—go and measure yourself elsewhere!"

In the second parabasis, the bird chorus sings an ode, declaring that they are gods and must be worshipped by mortals. They promise the judges rewards more precious than those that Paris received if they will award first prize to this play. A Messenger enters, seeking Pisthetairos, to whom he describes the beautiful city built by birds. with a top so wide that "even a pair of braggarts, / Theogenes and Proxenides, could drive / [a] pair of chariots past one another." But soon the Second Messenger arrives in despair because an unknown god has penetrated the city. This god turns out to be Iris, goddess of the rainbow and messenger of gods. Pisthetairos' immediate response to this crisis is to summon various birds armed with bow and slings. But the Chorus has a far better understanding of the sacrilege involved and immediately perceives that their new city is "on the brink of war." And when Pisthetairos' finally speaks directly to Iris, who has been sent by her father to tell the bird world that they must make sacrifice to the Olympian gods, she is dismissed contemptuously by Pisthetairos and warned not to annoy the birds. "The birds have now become new gods for men: / [i]t's they who need the sacrifice, not Zeus."

A Herald comes in and announces that many mortals now have the "bird madness" and wish to live in the new city. "O you who have founded this famous aerial city, / [y]ou do not know what honour you win from men." Next an old dithyrambic poet, named Kinesias, comes to ask Pisthetairos for wings. Kinesias is a dithyrambic poet, one who writes Greek choric hymns that were accompanied by mimic gestures, describing the adventures of Dionysus, the god of fertility and procreation. Though the etymology of the term is not certain, it was probably introduced into Greece in the early 7th century and, in its earliest form, was probably led by the leader of a band of revelers or group of dancers. Shortly before 500 B.C., it was introduced into Athens by Lasus of Hermione and recognized as one of the competitive subjects at various Athenian festivals. Kinesias is at first insulted and then offered the job of training the bird chorus. Kinesias rejects the job offer and immediately exits. No sooner is the poet gone than an informer appears, a man whose job it is to "travel round the islands as accuser, / [I]nformer too—" to ask for wings to help him perform his work more effectively, "to swoop and issue summonses." Pisthetairos' responds by calling the informer a "filthy devil" who should look for decent work instead.

The next visitor is Prometheus, who betrayed Zeus in befriending man and granting the gift of fire, and comes in masked lest Zeus recognize him. As usual, Prometheus is rebelling against the gods, and he offers his services as an informer. The renegade god tells Pisthetairos that because of the newly established city and its rulers, the Olympian gods have been deprived of the offerings of men. Indeed, they are starving. "Burnt offerings? None. We're fasting—like the women / /At the Thesmophoria." Furthermore, as a result of their hunger, the barbarian gods (the Triballians, the ancestral gods of Exekestides, a figure of supposedly dubious rights to Athenian citizenship) are threatening to declare war on Zeus. Thus, Zeus and the Triballians are planning to send ambassadors to make peace with the birds. Prometheus advises Pisthetairos to refuse to come to an agreement with the gods unless Zeus gives the sceptre back to the birds and grants the fair Princess to Pisthetairos. as his wife. Prometheus leaves with parasol in order to trick Zeus into taking him for a basket-carrier. After Prometheus leaves, Poseidon with a haughty air about him, Heracles wearing his club and lion skin with a gourmand's belly, and Triballus, one of the barbarous Thracian gods wearing an uncomfortable and unfamiliar Greek cloak, arrive to seek peace. Having discussed the matter for a while, they agree to Pistheteiros' terms, and the three gods depart. Pisthetairos is invited to Heaven to claim his two prizes. Pisthetairos now possesses the thunder and lightning of Zeus. As the Birds sing a marriage song, praising the marriage for bringing "felicity to our city," Pisthetairos invites them to follow him and his bride to the palace of Zeus. ❀

# List of Characters in
## *The Birds*

*Speaking Characters:*

**Euelpides:** an elderly Athenian

**Pisthetairos:** his companion, the same age

**Servant:** bird-slave of the Hoopoe

**Hoopoe:** the metamorphosed Tereus

**Chorus:** consists of twenty-four different species of birds

**Leader of the chorus**

**Priest**

**Poet**

**Oracle-Monger**

**Meton:** scientist and town planner

**Inspector:** Athenian imperial official

**Decree-Seller:** vendor of copies of state documents

**First Messenger:** a bird

**Second Messenger :** another bird

**Iris:** messenger of the gods

**Herald:** a bird, envoy from the Cloudcuckooland

**Father-Beater:** a disillusioned young man

**Kinesias:** Athenian lyric poet

**Informer:** a young Athenian who lives by malicious prosecutions

**Prometheus:** traitor to Zeus

**Poseidon:** leader of the divine assembly

**Heracles:** colleague of Poseidon's on the divine embassy

**Triballus:** a Thracian god, representative of barbarian deities

**Third Messenger :** a bird

*Silent Characters:*

**Flamingo; Mede:** an exotic bird, Second Hoopoe

**Prokne:** wife of the Hoopoe

**Gobbler:** an obese bird; **Raven:** a bird piper; Various **bird slaves**

**Basileia, a Princess:** a beautiful girl, symbolic incarnation of Zeus' power ✿

# Critical Views on
## *The Birds*

[William Arrowsmith is the general editor and translator of Nietzsche's *Unmodern Observations / Unzeitgemässe Betrachtungen* (1990) and translator and commentator for Eugenio Montale's *Occasioni* (1987). In the excerpt below from the introductory chapter to his translation of "The Birds," Arrowsmith discusses the dual themes of the idyllic world of rustic birds and their symbolic function of expressing man's desire to escape the problems of the real world.]

Nobody denies that *The Birds* is a masterpiece, one of the greatest comedies ever written and probably Aristophanes' finest. Splendidly lyrical, shot through with gentle Utopian satire and touched by the sadness of the human condition, its ironic gaiety and power of invention never flag; in no other play is Aristophanes' comic vision so comprehensively or lovingly at odds with his world.

But if the play is by common consent a great one, there is little agreement about what it means. Thus it has, with great ingenuity and small cogency, been interpreted as a vast, detailed comic allegory of the Sicilian expedition: Pisthetairos stands for Alkibiades; Hoopoe is the general Lamachos; the Birds are Athenians, the gods Spartans, and so on. Alternatively, the play has been viewed as Aristophanes' passionate appeal for the reform and renewal of Athenian public life under the leadership of the noble Pisthetairos, a true Aristophanic champion cut from the same cloth as Dikaiopolis in *The Acharnians.* Again, probably in revenge for so much unlikely ingenuity, it has been claimed that *The Birds* is best understood as a fantastic escapist extravaganza created as a revealing antidote to the prevalent folly of Athenian political life. And, with the exception of the word "escapist," this last view seems to me essentially correct. But whatever else *The Birds* may be, it is not escapist. ⟨. . .⟩

*The life of the Birds.* Like many Aristophanic comedies, *The Birds* takes its title from its chorus; but unlike, say, *Wasps,* which is based upon a simple simile (jurors are waspish: they buzz, swarm, sting, etc.) *Birds* and *Clouds* are titles around which cluster a great many traditional associations, idioms, and ideas. Thus in *Clouds* the chorus symbolizes the Murky Muse, that inflated, shining, insubstantial, and ephemeral power which inspires sophists, dithyrambic poets, prophets, and other pompous frauds. Similarly, in *Birds* there is the same natural clustering of association and standard idiom, and the associations are crucial to the play's understanding. On the most natural level, of course, the life of the Birds symbolizes precisely what one would expect: the simple, uncomplicated rustic life of peace. But behind this natural symbolism, deepening it and particularizing it, lies the chronic and pervasive escape-symbolism of late fifth-century Athens. In play after play of Euripides, for instance, chorus and characters alike, when confronted by the anguish of tragic existence, cry out their longing to escape, to be a bird, a fact of which Aristophanes makes extensive use, shaping his play around the symptomatic mortal infatuation with the birds. It is for this reason, this pervasive hunger for escape from intolerable existence which haunts tragedy and society alike, that Aristophanes makes his Birds address his audience with words of tragic pathos:

*O suffering mankind,*
        *lives of twilight,*
                *race feeble and fleeting,*
*like the leaves scattered!*
        *Pale generations,*
                *creatures of clay,*
*the wingless, the fading!*
        *Unhappy mortals,*
                *shadows in time,*
*flickering dreams!*
        *Hear us now,*
                *the ever-living Birds,*
*the undying,*
        *the ageless ones,*
                *scholars of eternity.*

And these lines in their turn look forward to the ironic apotheosis of the mortal Pisthetairos with which the play closes. Mankind's crazy comic dream is a wish-fulfillment darkened by death. But the dream survives.

My point is this: far from writing an escapist extravaganza, Aristo-phanes dramatizes the ironic fulfillment in divinity of the Athenian man who wants to escape. What begins as hunger for the simple life ends—such is the character of Athenians and true men—in world-conquest and the defeat of the gods; or it would end there, if only it could. This is the *hybris* of enterprise and daring, the trait from which no Athenian can ever escape. Aristophanes' irony is, I think, loving.

—William Arrowsmith, Introduction to *The Birds,* trans. William Arrowsmith (Ann Arbor: University of Michigan Press, 1969): pp. 1–3.

## Nan Dunbar on Analogue of Animal Behavior

[Nan Dunbar is the translator of two editions of *The Birds* (1995, 1998). In the excerpt below from his translation and introduction, Dunbar interprets "The Birds," as Aristophanes' interest in exploring a theme current in 5th century Greek life, namely a comparison of animal behavior with that of humans.]

*Birds,* the sixth extant play, was produced at the City Dionysia of 414, a spring festival, and won second prize (Hypothesis I $_9$); the first went to Ameipsias' *Revellers,* of which nothing is known, though the title suggests a jolly, undemanding piece, and the third to Phrynichos' *Recluse.* No play of Aristophanes has aroused more con-troversy over its interpretation than *Birds.* Alone among his extant plays it concentrates on a non-human world; it has a chorus of birds, and the life and world of birds—their rich variety of songs and calls, their enviable freedom of movement, their habits and habitats, their appalling sufferings at the hands of the enemy, Man, and their resulting hostility—are vigorously exploited by the poet for both dramatic and poetic ends ⟨. . .⟩.

⟨. . .⟩ Some scholars, notably Gilbert Murray (*Aristophanes* (Oxford, 1933). ch. VI), have seen *Birds* as a comedy of pure escape from harsh reality into poetic fantasy; but this interpretation rests upon an inac-curate view of the contemporary situation in Athens. Although there must have been some tension and anxiety in Athens in 414, with the great armada far off in Sicily and with continuing reverberations from the previous summer of the major religious scandals of vandalized Herms and parodied Mysteries, yet the current situation, military and political, was certainly not one of disaster or gloom from which a longing to escape would be natural. The defection to Sparta of Alkibiades after his arrest was indeed a blow, but no decisive victory or defeat had yet occurred in Sicily when *Birds* was produced, and Aristophanes may have fully approved of the expedition.

Aristophanes' depiction of life with the birds, free from the pressures and restrictions that affect humans (155–61, 753–68, 785–800, 1088–1101) is, as far as we can tell, a highly original variant on an ancient theme, the nostalgic myth of life in the reign of Kronos, father of Zeus, when nobody had to work for a living because all good things freely provided themselves. This theme of the lost life of bliss, which appears first in Hesiod, *WD* III–20, had been caricatured in Old Comedy before Ar., but we do not know how it was related to the plots. ⟨. . .⟩

By the late 5th c. any treatment of this theme, even in comedy, was likely to be affected by current intellectual arguments about the basis of human ethics, i.e. whether ethical rules based on tradition are contrary to nature and therefore not binding; see introd. to 753–68. Aristophanes may have been influenced by his competitor Pherekrates' recent treatment (420 BC) of the related theme of men living free from all the usual restrictions of society in his *Wild Men;* but from the scanty ancient evidence for this comedy, particularly Plato in *Prt.* 327 C–D, it is clear that Pherekrates' play depicted such a life as horrible, and infinitely less tolerable than the much criticized life in Athens. An interesting parallel may have occurred in Phrynichos' *Recluse,* which came third in the contest in which *Birds* was second (Hyp. I 9–10); two fragments (19–20) suggest that the chief character has withdrawn completely from Athenian society, as Peisetairos and Euelpides propose at the outset, but unlike them has become a recluse. Aristophanes exploits for his own comedy a potentially more attractive element in contemporary arguments about nature and tradition—the discussions of the relevance of animal behaviour to questions of human ethical norms (755–9 nn.), and he has filled it with charm as well as humour by choosing for his illustrative animals the colourful, varied, and melodious birds.

—Nan Dunbar, *Aristophanes's Birds* (Oxford: Clarendon Press, 1998): pp. 2, 6–7.

# THOMAS GELZER ON THE PHANTASTIC ELEMENTS

[Thomas Gelzer is the author of *Lamella Bernensis: ein spä-tantikes Goldamulett mit christlichem Exorzismus* (1999) and *Le Classicisme a Rome, aux 1ers siecles avant et apres J.-C. neuf exposes suivis de discussions* (1979). In the excerpt below from his article, "Some Aspects of Aristophanes' Dramatic Art in the *Birds*," Gelzer discusses the ways in which the Prologue introduces the many phantastic elements within the play.]

⟨. . .⟩ It is of course difficult to describe Aristophanes' dramatic art in terms appropriate to tragedy and New Comedy, types of drama which have much in common with Old Comedy and yet are so very different; I propose therefore to start not from abstract concepts but from a study of the way in which his dramatic technique works in practice; in the short time available I would like to look in detail at a few concrete examples of its use in the *Birds*.

Right from the beginning the Prologue gives us an introduction of a masterly kind to the phantastic atmosphere of the piece. The dramatic means which are employed in the later parts of the comedy, with a great profusion of people, things, and musical and metrical forms, are already present in essence here.

In front of a stage-set which as yet betrays nothing of what is concealed behind it, two old men are moving around in uncertain direction in the orchestra: tired, heavily laden, and lost. Only trees (1), a wood (92), undergrowth (202 ff., 256), rocks (54) are obviously visible—a wilderness, but no house, no entrance, no trace of any inhabitants whatsoever, and no indication of where they might come from. All this is, on the contrary, what the two men are themselves looking for, and what they discover only after an ostentatiously produced detour. The audience is therefore at first totally uncertain about what they are being given to look at, and the emphasised lack of certainty about what they are given to see at the beginning, and about the stage décor and the appearance and movements of the actors, arouses a general curiosity about what must be going to transpire here. By these means Aristophanes establishes in a masterly way, right from the beginning, a sense of anticipation which carries the audience along. The audience knows, of course, that the uncertainty will not last, but that this will be a play in which actors and a chorus, under generally well-known conditions, and in forms which it knows of old, will present a comedy. The especially wide divergence between this quite particular expectation on the one hand, and the possibilities of foreseeing how it will be fulfilled this time on the other, creates a tension which stimulates the curiosity of the audience to a remarkable degree. The way in which the information, essential for understanding the comedy, is revealed step by step, compels the audience to concentrate on virtually every word which is said, and creates a readiness to follow, almost without knowing it, Aristophanes' train of thought—and this readiness is then the basic means, by which the audience is drawn into Aristophanes' comic inventions. Their dramatic penetrating force is intensified by the economy with which he plays with this expectation, now accelerating, now decelerating.

At first the audience's attention is directed towards the two birds, the crow and the jackdaw, whose directions the two men are following in their erratic wanderings. By this means the audience learns, it is true, why they are proceeding in such an apparently random zig-zag course—but not, on the other hand, where they are going and to what purpose. Above all, however, the two confess that they have no idea where they are (9 f.). Attention is therefore drawn additionally to the mysterious deserted wood; but its significance and identity are still withheld: the audience's curiosity is excited even more strongly. But then one of the characters addresses the spectators directly in two small monologues (13 ff., 27 ff.). Now the audience is entitled to expect that it will be put straight in the picture, in the usual way of Prologues, about the situation and the purpose of the whole enterprise. Well, it learns something at least: first the starting-point and destination of the journey on which the two are engaged. They have bought the two birds in Athens, in the bird-market, as guides to take them to Tereus, who has been transformed from a man into a hoopoe—so the motive for their vague search is revealed. Then the reason for their journey is made clear: they have left their city in order to escape the excessive litigation. Thereby they are identified as true-born Athenians, and the luggage which they carry becomes meaningful. The purpose of the basket, the pot, and the branches of myrtle, as equipment for the sacrifice at a new foundation, is not explicitly stated, but any spectator with his wits about him can deduce it from the circumstances. One learns too that Tereus is not the ultimate aim of their journey, but is only to be a source of information to tell them from his experience where they might find a ⟨*topos apragmon*⟩ in which ultimately to settle. What they have in mind to do there is not yet let out.

—Thomas Gelzer, "Some Aspects of Aristophanes' Dramatic Art in the *Birds*," *Bulletin of the Institute of Classical Studies* 23 (1976): pp. 2–3.

## STEPHEN HALLIWELL ON DUAL THEMES OF POLITICS AND MYTH

[Stephen Halliwell is the author of "Philosophical Rhetoric or Rhetorical Philosophy? The Strange Case of Isocrates" (1997) and "The Challenge of Rhetoric to Political and Ethical Theory in Aristotle" (1996). In the excerpt below from his introductory chapter in his translation of the plays, Halliwell discusses "The Birds" in terms of the dual themes of the contemporary polis and the mythic ability of humans to be transformed into birds.]

At the heart of Aristophanes' and Old Comedy's unpredictability lies the exercise of fantasy, which in this context might be defined as the unfettered manipulation of materials furnished by the full gamut of both experience and imagination. One way of gaining a preliminary sense of how Aristophanic fantasy operates is to consider a characteristic opening from one of his plays. Let us take as our example *Birds*, which starts in a rural setting (probably indicated, but only sketchily, in the original staging) where two elderly Athenians, their age and apparently rather ordinary social status indicated by their masks and costumes, are staggering around with birds on their wrists and with a variety of baggage and paraphernalia. They appear bewildered and lost, and so too, though with more amusement, might an audience be. For what are these old men doing? Their baggage probably suggests a long journey, perhaps even 'emigration', as well as the possibility of a sacrifice. But why are they using chained birds for orientation? As soon as Euelpides tells us that these are birds bought from a named Athenian market-trader, yet purchased with a view to finding Tereus (13–15), we are faced by a binary frame of reference that is quintessentially Aristophanic. We are required not only to accept simultaneously, but also to allow to merge into one another, the real-life logic of the contemporary polis, where ordinary birds are for sale every day on market stalls, and the world of Greek myth, within which metamorphosis from man to bird is possible. We are invited, in other words, into a special comic universe, which both is and is not continuous with the Athens of the audience.

The nature of this comic universe is gradually revealed in more detail when Euelpides eventually turns to the audience at 27 ff. (an extra-dramatic gesture itself characteristic of comic freedom) to explain the situation. Euelpides and Peisetairos are ageing Athenians looking for an escape from the oppressive reality of the city, especially its culture of litigation. That they are so old and yet prepared to turn to such a far-fetched means of release from their frustrations is itself significantly improbable. Aristophanes repeatedly associates the transformations effected by comic fantasy with elderly protagonists who become symbols of prodigious daring and/or rejuvenation (cf. *Acharnians, Knights, Clouds, Wasps, Peace, Wealth*). Moreover, as characters these people are thoroughly adapted to the absurdity of the setting. They do not speak as consistent individuals with whom reasonably predictable dealings would be possible, but as figures whose voices constantly shift tone and level, now reflecting elements of social reality (concern over debts, and so on), now engaging in the artificial joke exchanges of a comic double act (e.g. 54–60), and generally displaying a capacity to tolerate incongruity in themselves as well as around them. This quality, which is familiar to us from the behaviour of stand-up comedians and clowns, and which is a defining characteristic of Aristophanic characterization, can best be described as quasi-*improvisatory*. It leaves the impression that, to invert a principle of Aristotle's, the figures often say what the playwright wants and not what (in realistic terms) the situation plausibly calls for. It is the freedom of Aristophanic fantasy which gives rise to this malleability of persona (as of plot), so that many of the leading characters in the plays are constructed more by aggregation than integration.

—Stephen Halliwell, *Aristophanes: Birds, Lysistrata, Assembly-Women and Wealth* (Oxford and New York: Clarendon Press, 1997): pp. xxii–xxiv.

[Gilbert Murray is the author of "Hamlet and Orestes: A Study in Traditional Types" (1996) and *The Classical Tradition in Poetry* (1968). In the excerpt below from the chapter entitled "The Plays of Escape," Murray discusses the status of birds in terms of their human and political analogues.]

Peithetairos expounds the ancient rights of the Birds. They were once kings, a claim which he illustrates by many examples; and now he can show them how to recover their kingdom. The Birds listen spell-bound. They are melted to tears by his description of the way in which they are now treated, pelted like madmen, driven out of the temples where others have sanctuary, snared, limed, caged, eaten and, as if that was not enough, drowned in thick sauces! He shows in detail how they can make or mar mankind; how they can rule much better than the gods who have usurped their throne. The Birds are wild with enthusiasm and accept the plan. The two men are taken into the Hoopoe's dwelling in the rock to be provided with wings.

The Birds left alone break suddenly into a lyrical summons to the Nightingale ⟨. . .⟩

'Dear one, tawny-throat, best-beloved of birds . . . you have come, you have come, we have seen you.'

Her fluting is to lead their song, which then begins in long anapaests. It is a great cosmogony in the style of Orpheus or Musaeus, addressed by 'the Birds of the Sky, who live for ever, ageless and deathless, and filled with immortal thoughts, to the dimly existing tribes of men, little-doing, moulded of clay, strengthless multitudes that fade as the leaf.' ⟨. . .⟩

These birds, like Keats's nightingale, were 'not born for death'; no hungry generations trod them down, such as were now harassing Athens. They explain how in the beginning of things the Birds were born of Erôs and Chaos, how they are older than the Olympian gods, how in spite of their dethronement they still guide and direct human life, and how all signs and omens are 'birds'. Later in the parabasis they explain how their City will be an asylum for the misfits of the world; for father-beaters—since birds freely fight their fathers—for fugitives, for slaves and outcasts and barbarians, and for all, one might say, who are ashamed or unhappy among men. Then they expatiate on the usefulness of wings, chiefly for getting out of the theatre if you are bored or have other business, but also for climbing in the world, like Dieitrephes, the basket-seller, on his wings of wicker.

As often in Aristophanes, there is here a rush of real feeling and beauty, quickly apologized for and turned off with a laugh. And curiously enough, the feeling turns out to be based on something more than mere fancy; for the birds, as objects of worship in the Aegean area, were really older than the Olympian gods. Their sanctity goes back to pre-Hellenic times. Birds were in Greece, bringing thunder and rain, or giving signs to prophets, long before the anthropomorphic band of warlike Olympians descended from the northern forests: the eagle and the swan before Zeus, the owl before Athena, the dove before Aphrodite. There must have been more relics of pre-Hellenic cults extant in Aristophanes' time than we generally realize; but none the less it was a remarkable feat of imaginative guess-work, aided perhaps by some special love of birds in themselves, that enabled Aristophanes to catch this glimpse of a truth so long hidden from the generations after him.

—Gilbert Murray, "The Plays of Escape," *Aristophanes: A Study* (New York: Oxford University Press, 1933): pp. 145–48.

## ERICH SEGAL ON THE *THE BIRDS*

[Erich Segal is the editor of *Oxford Readings in Aristophanes* (1996) and the author of *Roman Laughter: The Comedy of Plautus* (1968). In the excerpt below from his chapter entitled "The *Birds:* The Uncensored Fantasy," Segal discusses the play as a literary masterpiece which brilliantly weaves the etymological roots of comedy with the current political situation in Athens.]

The *Birds* takes comedy as far as it can go. It dramatizes, with a unique combination of the lyre and phallus, the fullest expression of the comic dream. In a word, it is Aristophanes' masterpiece. While producing a work of transcendent brilliance, he also captured the historical moment at which it was composed. Aristophanes can thus share Ben Jonson's praise of Shakespeare: he is at once the "soul of an age" as well as "not for an age but for all time."

In the summer before the *Birds* was presented at the Great Dionysia (414 B.C.), Athens undertook, at the urging of Alcibiades, the most audacious venture in the long Peloponnesian War, launching a vast armada—according to Thucydides, the most magnificent force ever assembled by a Greek City—to conquer Sicily and sever Sparta from her western allies. It was ultimately to prove a disaster, but at the time of the play, the Athenians were still drunk with hope and dreams of power. Sicily was El Dorado to them, a land of infinite wishes. Like Hamlet, they "ate the air, promise crammed." ⟨...⟩

In the *Birds,* Aristophanes is not necessarily mocking his country's imperialistic urges directly. Nevertheless, he perfectly captures the feeling that was in the air. In Thucydides' account of the Athenians' mood at this time, the note of the being "drunk with hope" (*euelpides*) is sounded several times. Small wonder that Aristophanes has named one of his wandering heroes Euelpides, and the other Peisetaerus ("Friend-Persuader").

Moreover, there was a special phallic dimension to the events of 415. As mentioned earlier, the Athenians had been placing priapic icons of Hermes outside their front doors for centuries to ward off the evil eye. The night before the fleet sailed, these statutes were mutilated by unknown vandals. Thucydides recalls the shock of the Athenians, who regarded it as "a very grave incident." *Birds* is an artistic reaction to what Aristophanes elsewhere refers to as the "Hermes-choppers." For although the *Birds* is in one sense a traditional comedy—the hero's goal is not unlike that of Dicaeopolis or even Strepsiades—on a more fundamental level the play is about, in no uncertain terms, the reinvigoration of the phallus. And on a more universal level, its psychological significance goes back to the dawn of man—a fantasy which even predates its expression in ritual (which is why the poet is "for all time").

The general theme is the acquisition of wings by men—itself a great sexual metaphor. Freud explains the erotic dream symbolism of "flying fantasies" and the

> remarkable characteristic of the male organ which enables
> it to rise up in defiance of the laws of gravity, one of the

> phenomena of erection . . . But dreams can symbolize erection in yet another, far more expressive manner. They can treat the sexual organ as the essence of the dreamer's whole person and make him himself fly.

It should come as no surprise then that the Greek word for "wing" also served as a euphemism for phallus. After all, "bird" is still used to refer to the male member in the slang of many modern languages. Besides the English "cock" and "flip the bird," the Greek idiom is matched in French by *le petit oiseau*, in Italian by *l'uccello*, in Spanish by *pajarito*, as well as by the German verb *vögeln* ("to bid," that is, to have intercourse). In both Greece and Rome, birds were lovers' gifts. One thinks of the vivid connotation of the sparrow with which Catallus delighted Lesbia—until it "died." ⟨. . .⟩

Comedy, as we have seen, was born of the *komos*, engendered by the same two forces that the Birds will claim as their parents in the Birdogony of the *parabasis*: Eros and Chaos. Alongside it marched the bawdy banter of the phallic procession, which ultimately made its way to the stage. These primal elements are nowhere more clearly preserved than in this comedy. Indeed, the play concludes with a triumphant procession–a phallic play within a play—this time on a much grander scale than the one we saw in *Archanians*. *The Birds* is thus the ultimate destination toward which *ta phallika* had been leading for centuries, and it perfectly reflects the orgiastic mood of the Athenians before the defeat of the Sicilian Expedition. ⟨. . .⟩

As the play nears its conclusion, the chorus-leader calls the chorus to celebrate Zeus' "awesome thunderbolt" (*deinon keraunon*) in the most elegant lyric strains. The bolt of Zeus now seems to have replaced Peisetaerus as the central character. The bolt has been described as both "winged" and the "firebearing spear" (*enchos pyrphoron*). Like any good wedding hymn, the song that ends the play is emphatically ithyphallic. The image of the phallus overshadows the individual people, as it did the celebrants in the ancient phallic procession. It is the emblem of how Peisetaerus feels as he approaches the wedding-bed of Basileia.

> —Erich Segal, "The *Birds*: The Uncensored Fantasy," *The Death of Comedy* (Cambridge, Mass. and London: Harvard University Press, 2001): pp. 85–88, 96.

# Plot Summary of
## *The Clouds*

The original version of *The Clouds* was presented in March 423 B.C., at the Great Dionysia at which Aristophanes fully expected to win first prize. Unfortunately, *The Clouds* came in third, the first prize going to Kratinos for *Pytine* (*The Wineflask*) and the runner up going to Ameipsias for *Konnos*. Needless to say, Aristophanes was very disappointed. He had considered this play to be his finest work to date and decided to revise it, perhaps to get a second consensus among his readers and to respond to his critics. Thus, the only existing copy of the play is the revised version of some three or four years following its original staging, and this revised version was probably never meant to be performed. Nevertheless, *The Clouds* is a stunning masterpiece, a brilliant satire of 5th century Athenian society focusing on an important educational issue, and its affect on the legal system. The relevant educational debate is that of the New Education which had a vocational agenda which stressed the requisite legal and verbal skills vital to the conduct of Athenian imperialism versus the Old Education which emphasized Music and Gymnastics, concentrating on the inward man and the soul as well as the mind, in order to form a disciplined reason within a disciplined body. All of this is presented within an extremely preposterous and absurd framework which assigns it entirely to the realm of comic distortion and absurdity. The prevailing concern in this play is that of rhetoric, which in Aristophanes' time meant public speaking and the means used to persuade the audience. In the ancient world, rhetoric was considered to be a powerful tool with the potential to do great harm if used to distort the truth in an effort to construct a convincing argument. Aristophanes is equally as interested in the judicial ramifications of using language "to overcome the truth by telling lies." He is likewise aware that the Athenians were a litigious society and never misses a chance to call attention to this. More specifically, *The Clouds* is a searing indictment of a particular group of individuals known as sophists.

The sophists were itinerant professors of higher education, their name originating with the notion of sage or expert, which in the 5th century B.C. was applied to various teachers who traveled throughout the Greek world, delivering both popular lectures and specialized training in a broad range of topics. It is important to bear in mind, however, that the sophists were neither a school nor a movement, there was no common set of precepts, and they were never an organized group. Their interests included a wide spectrum of topics such as philosophy, mathematics and the "social" sciences of history, geography and speculative anthropology. They pioneered a systematic study of the techniques of persuasive argument which relied on the study of language within a variety of contexts such as literary criticism, grammar and semantics. The sophists indeed aroused a strong response from both their proponents and their detractors, the former group acknowledging the importance of effective public speaking as a guarantee of professional success, while the latter group denounced the sophists' subversion of morality and traditional values, mainly that of religious beliefs. In a word, some considered the sophists to be a great threat to the prevailing social order in their ability to distort the truth through a skillful manipulation of language. Indeed, *The Clouds* is also a subversive play advocating internal strife in the service of invalidating the powers of the Olympians gods. And, here, Aristophanes uses Socrates as the prototypical Sophist although, ironically, Socrates in fact had attacked their practices.

Socrates (469–399 B.C.) was an important Athenian public figure who occupied a central role in the intellectual debate in the middle and late 5th century Athens. Both his philosophy and his personality reached a large audience primarily through the dialogues written by his associates, and in which he was placed as the central figure. Socrates adhered to the belief that wisdom and virtue were one and the same, holding that if a man knows what is right, he will necessarily act that way. Conversely, if a man chooses the wrong course of action, this is attributable to the fact that he does not know any better. Interestingly, Socrates' moral seriousness is directly opposite to his urbane personality which enjoyed good food and company. Nevertheless, in 399, Socrates was put on trial for impiety for introducing new gods and corrupting his young disciples. The immediate cause of his death was his drinking a cup of hemlock.

In the end, the truth about Socrates' character depends on the way he is constructed by several "biographers," namely Aristophanes, Plato and Xenophon. Most importantly, it was held by Plato and Xenophon that Aristophanes' slanderous portrayal of Socrates in

*The Clouds* as a morally irresponsible philosopher who taught his students to "make the weaker argument stronger," lead to his condemnation and execution by the state. Furthermore, Socrates differed from the character Aristophanes draws in many important respects: he did not accept money for teaching; he refused to found a school; his extraordinary modesty is demonstrated in his claim that he knew nothing; and he did not accept the theories about natural science popular in his time. Furthermore, Socrates devoted his life to seeking the truth, and, thus, he is in sharp contrast with the sophistic interest in effective argument rather than in the true nature of a problem. Aristophanes' image of Socrates is a distorted one, though it is not clear whether this distortion results from personal animosity or artistic necessity. And, with respect to the latter, it is important to remember that some of Aristophanes' "slanders" are conventionally driven since Old Comedy was heir to the earlier *komos*, a comic tradition based on invective and abuse.

The scene opens with two houses in the background, one is the home of Strepsiades, and the other the "Thinkery" of Socrates. Strepsiades, a debt dodger (whose name is derived from the Greek word for turning and twisting), is an old man, lying in bed unable to sleep because he is troubled by the debts of his son who has spent a great deal of money on his primary concern—chariot racing. In another bed, is Strepsiades' son, Pheidippides (whose name has the etymological suggestion of the Scrimping Aristocrat), talking in his sleep about the chariot races and ranting against a losing horse. "Philo, you fouled me! Keep in your own lane!" All this while Strepsiades thinks back on the happy days of his youth before his marriage when he lived an untroubled, simple life in the country, "the sweetest life on earth." After his marriage to a haughty woman of the city, all his troubles begin. However, these meditations quickly end with Strepsiades suddenly hitting upon a strategy to solve the problem of his son's debts. He suggests that Pheidippides enroll in the "Thinkery," Socrates' school, where for a certain sum a man can learn to lie so well that he can win the lawsuits which will inevitably result from his financial mismanagement. "[F]or a fee—of course / They offer a course called The Technique of Winning Lawsuits." But when Pheidippides expresses his unwillingness to enroll because attendance at school will spoil his suntan, "they'd scrape the tan right off my face," Strepsiades has no other alternative but to take the course himself. He rushes off to the "Thinkery" and knocks at the door whereupon a disciple of Socrates scolds Strepsiades for having disturbed a great scientific discovery" and caused it to "miscarry." The old man is then told about the strange and complicated problems that Socrates' students are involved in. "Just a minute ago Socrates was questioning Chairephon / about the number of fleafeet a flea could broad jump." While he observes some of these students, he finally he sees Socrates in a basket suspended from the ceiling to whom he calls out. Socrates explains that he must let his mind associate with the upper air in order to have lofty thoughts. "You see, / only by being suspended aloft, by dangling / my mind in the heavens and mingling my rare thought / with the ethereal air, could I ever achieve strict / scientific accuracy in my vast survey of the empyrean."

Strepsiades tells the master of his intention to learn to speak effectively so he can reason with his creditors and thus avoid payment of his debts. "I want instruction in your second Logic, / you know the one—the get-away-without-paying argument." In response, Socrates vows to effect a transformation, turning Strepsiades into "the perfect flower of orators, / a consummate, blathering, tinkling rascal." Socrates then prays to the Air and the Clouds, the goddesses "of men of leisure and philosophers," whom he adores, and soon the Chorus of Clouds enters "in a mist of verbal fluff." Socrates explains to Strepsiades that these are the goddesses who come to the indolent; they are responsible for discourse and all the arts of persuasion. The Clouds, who support sophists, and a variety of other charlatans, are the only real deities, the others, traditional Olympians, are declared figments of the imagination. Since Zeus does not exist, it is the clouds that create rain, thunder and lightning, thus usurping Zeus' authority. "The proof is incontrovertible. / For instance, / have you ever yet seen rain when you didn't see a cloud?" Socrates then goes on to tell Strepsiades that he must follow the example of the master and honor no gods except Chaos, the Clouds and the Tongue. Strepsiades agrees. "Ladies, if all you require / is hard work, insomnia, worry, endurance, and a stomach / that eats anything, why, have no fear." The leader of the Chorus asks Strepsiades what he wants, and he replies that he wishes to surpass all other Greeks in the gift of speech, with "muscular tongue," to "outrace the whole of Hellas." However, when he is granted the gift of eloquence, Strepsiades reveals that his agenda is a very limited one. He is not interested in political power for he wants only the ability to deceive his creditors, which is to say courtroom eloquence. "All I want is to escape the clutches / of my creditors." The Leader then tells Strepsiades that he must entrust himself to the Sophists, and Strepsiades agrees to do so in the hope that he will then appear to be arrogant, "a welshre, a cheater, a bastard, a phoney and a bum." The Chorus is delighted with its new pupil. "Ah, here's a ready spirit, undaunted, unafraid."

After Socrates and Strepsiades enter the "Thinkery," in order to initiate Strepsiades into this "solemn philosophical institution," the Chorus speaks to the audience, in the first person, as the poet himself, declaring *The Clouds* to be his best play, "my comedy / comes to you / relying upon herself and her poetry / . . . I am the poet, her adoring father," encouraging the audience to share his view. Following this commentary, Socrates returns very irritated with the vulgarity and stupidity of Strepsiades, "such a bungling, oblivious, brainless imbecile," who comes out of the "Thinkery" carrying a mattress. Strepsiades proceeds to lie down on his bed, while Socrates continues to lecture him. But Strepsiades remains firm in stating that his only interest is in learning the art of false reasoning so that he can overcome his creditors. "Teach me your Immoral Logic." Socrates finally loses patience with the old man and sends him away, advising him to send his son, Pheidippides, to the "Thinkery."

When Strepsiades proceeds to summon Pheidippides to the Thinkery, he reluctantly obeys his father, although he views the teachings of the sophists to be sheer madness. There his teachers are to be Philosophy (Just Discourse) and Sophistry (Unjust Discourse), two figures who enter the stage in great, gilded cages. They are presented as part human from the shoulders down, and part bird from the neck up and, as the cages are opened, they are already engaged in a quarrel as to who is superior. Philosophy is on the side of truth and justice, which requires obedience, modesty, discipline, and physical training, and which teaches the traditional values and respect for elders. "I propose to speak of the Old Education, as it flourished / once / beneath my tutelage." Sophistry, on the other hand, argues for the New Education which approves of physical pleasure, including hot baths and sexual indulgence and teaches rhetorical tricks for winning an argument or a lawsuit, even when in the wrong. "But follow me / my boy, / and obey your nature to the full; romp, play, and laugh / without a scruple in the world." At the end of this contest, Sophistry wins the argument through his trickery and becomes the teacher of Phidippides. Philosophy then returns to his cage and exits the stage.

The Chorus now turns to the audience and tells the judges of the contest for comedy, in which Aristophanes is competing, that if they award the prize to this play, the Clouds will reward them by caring for their crops. "First of all, when the season sets, / For Spring and plowing time has come, we guarantee each / judge's fields / the top priority in rain." Shortly thereafter, Strepsiades returns to the "Thinkery" to find out what his son has been learning. Socrates praises Pheidippides, saying now Strepsiades "can evade any legal action" he wishes. Pheidippides soon appears and shows how well he has learned the tricks of the Sophists and, through this newly acquired virtuosity, Strepsiades is able to get rid of his two creditors, Pasias and Amynias.

A little later Strepsiades rushes out of his house, bellowing with great pain and terror, followed by Pheidippides who is threatening his father with a murderous stick. The two have been quarreling over the merits of the playwright, Aeschylus, whom Strepsiades has branded a "colossal bore" and that quarrel has become violent. The newly-schooled Pheidippides, using sophistic trickery, insists that it is right to beat his father since Strepsiades had previously beat his son. When Strepsiades cannot refute Pheidippides' arguments that he can now advocate "new legislation granting sons the power to / inflict corporal punishments upon wayward fathers," the young main claims it is also right to beat his mother. Strepsiades is now convinced that Socrates and the Clouds have caused all his trouble. The Clouds, however, tell him that his own corruption has brought him to his present disgrace. "Because this is what we are, / the insubstantial Clouds men build their hopes upon, / shining tempters formed of air, symbols of desire." Strepsiades admits he should not have cheated his creditors. His faith in the old gods is now restored, and he and the emaciated, ghostlike slaves set fire to the "Thinkery" of Socrates. ❁

# List of Characters in
## *The Clouds*

**Strepsiades:**  father of Pheidippides

**Pheidippides:**  a playboy

**Xanthias:**  a slave bearing a common servile name

**Socrates**

**Students of Socrates**

**Chorus of Clouds**

**Koryphaios:**  a chorus leader

**Aristophanes**

**Philosopher**

**Sophistry**

**Pasias:**  creditor of Strepsiades

**Amynias:**  a creditor of Strepsiades

**Chairephon:**  a pupil and disciple of Socrates, his scrawniness and emaciated pallor are forever ridiculed by Aristophanes.

**Slaves, students, witnesses, etc.** ❀

# Critical Views on
## *The Clouds*

WILLIAM ARROWSMITH ON LITERARY ASPECTS

[William Arrowsmith is the general editor and translator of Nietzsche's *Unmodern Observations / Unzeitgemässe Betrachtungen* (1990) and translator and commentator for *Eugenio Montale's Occasioni* (1987). In the excerpt below from the introduction to his translation of *The Clouds,* Arrowsmith discusses the literary aspects of the *Clouds* and Aristophanes' parody of the sophistic teachers of his time.]

Even in its present form, revised for readers rather than for the stage, *The Clouds* is visibly a masterpiece, a play of wonderful, ragging satire, tilted so expertly toward the preposterous and the absurd that its effect is wholly and unmistakably comic. We have, in fact, almost a *reductio ad absurdum* of the satirical intent, satire become so *buffa* and burlesque that its characters and targets, by sheer exaggeration and incongruity, survive as directly comic. In short, a splendid play, beautifully sustained and shaped, and everywhere guided by Aristophanes' genius for comic distortion and his cunning of absurdity. If not the funniest play he ever wrote, it is certainly the cleverest: clever in construction and plot, clever in its exploitation of incongruities, clever in polemic and wit. Almost, perhaps, too clever for its own good. But for Aristophanes these very qualities of cleverness and wit were precisely what made *The Clouds* superior to his own previous work and that of his "cheap and vulgar rivals": for their slapstick of situation and crude horseplay he here substitutes the ludicrous slapstick of the intellect and the better horseplay of poetry and imagination. In its structure too *The Clouds* is an improvement. Unusually tight and coherent, at least by Aristophanic standards, its action is all of a piece, a continuously unfolding plot, written to be performed by a small cast, and singlemindedly devoted to the pursuit of its quarry. If it lacks the miraculous violence and vigor of *The Knights* or the exuberance of *The Acharnians,* it makes up for those qualities by the greater clarity and economy of its design and the pure lyricism of its poetry. Until *The Birds,* there is nothing in Aristophanes to match the loveliness of the poetry here assigned to the Chorus of Clouds as it enters. In this play, for the first time, we catch a glimpse of that exquisite tension between slapstick and poetry, the obscene and the sublime, which was Aristophanes' major individual contribution to comedy and which lies at the heart of his two greatest lyrical comedies, *The Birds* and *The Frogs*.

At first blush the improbable victim of *The Clouds* seems to be the philosopher Sokrates. But actually Aristophanes is deliberately exploiting Sokrates here as a convenient comic representative of the sophistic corruption which is the play's real subject. In the illustration of that corruption, Sokrates is nothing more than the poet's cipher, a curious catchpaw of those enormous cultural polarities (Old and New, Tradition and Innovation, Country and City, Peace and War, Poetry and Prose, Custom and Logic, etc.) which Aristophanes loved to elaborate and which he presented in play after play as locked in a life-and-death struggle for the soul of Athens. Whether Aristophanes privately believed that Sokrates was a sophist or presented him that way for its comic and preposterous effect, we shall never know. But for the purposes of the play, Sokrates is merely a genial polemical emblem of the sophistic movement—if that extraordinary simultaneous flowering of individual genius, crankery, "educationism," and fraud can be called a movement at all. For Aristophanes such distinctions are academic, and to his mind the sophists are a movement only because they are something worse, a conspiracy of charlatans and humbugs. Distinctions of doctrine and belief are totally disregarded. Jumbled together in ludicrous proximity and then stuffed into the mouth of Sokrates are the doctrines of Protagoras, the pre-Socratics generally, Anaxagoras, Diagoras, Gorgias, Prodikos, and perhaps Thrasymachos. It is grotesque—and hilarious. It is polemic on the grand scale, contemptuous of niceties, careless of reputations, unfair, Procrustean, and passionately loyal to its central perception. Addressed to, and exploiting, the average man's ridiculous stereotype of philosophy and science, it remains an honest and uncompromising play.

—William Arrowsmith, Introduction to *The Clouds*, trans. William Arrowsmith (Ann Arbor: University of Michigan Press, 1969): pp. 2–3.

[Kenneth James Dover is the author of *Greek and the Greeks: Language, Poetry, Drama* (1987) and *Greek Popular Morality in the Time of Plato and Aristotle* (1974). In the excerpt below from his introduction to *Clouds,* Dover discusses some ways in which this play differs from some of the other Aristophanic comedies and the significance of Strepsiades' name.]

Our conception of the typical Old Comedy is, in part, formed by the resemblances between *Acharnians, Peace, Birds, Lysistrata,* and *Ecclesiazusae.* In each of these plays a bold, pertinacious, resourceful hero (or heroine) effects and exploits a triumph of fantasy over reality; we enter and enjoy, with a 'suspension of disbelief', a realm in which the familiar mechanisms of nature and society operate only when the poet wishes them to do so. ⟨. . .⟩

*Clouds* strikes a different note. The 'hero', Strepsiades, is stupid and excitable, never truly resourceful, never in control of the situation, and at the end pitiable. He believes that he has solved his problem, the lawsuits with which his creditors threaten him, by having his son, Pheidippides, educated in rhetoric in the school of Socrates; but one of the lessons which Pheidippides learns is reckless contempt for his father. Strepsiades revenges himself on Socrates by brute force, burning down the school; but he has still to live with his son and his creditors, who are now his implacable enemies because of the insolence and violence with which he has treated them. The Chorus, which in *Knights, Peace, Lysistrata,* and *Ecclesiazusae* is well disposed to the hero or heroine from first to last, and in *Acharnians, Wasps,* and *Birds* is converted from initial hostility in the course of the play, has a strange and equivocal role in *Clouds.* It encourages Strepsiades in the first part of the play, turns by degrees to moralizing, and emerges at the end as a stern agent of divine retribution. Like Knemon in Menander's *Dyskolos* (703 ff.), Strepsiades at the end repents of the moral error without which there would have been no comedy. ⟨. . .⟩

*Names.* We first learn in 134 that the old man who spoke the first words of the play is Strepsiades, son of Pheidon, of the deme Kikynna; we have already learned (65 ff.) that he wanted to call his son 'Pheidonides', after his own father, but settled for 'Pheidippides' after a dispute with his wife. None of these names is intrinsically humorous—indeed, they are less so than many names which we encounter on Athenian fifth-century casualty-lists. The Theban wrestler whose victory is celebrated by Pindar in *I. 7* was called 'Strepsiadas', and his uncle bore the same name; the name 'Strepsippidas' occurs at Lebadeia in the third century B.C. (*IG* vii. 3068.7). ⟨...⟩

Strepsiades is to be imagined as past, or nearly past, the age limit for military service; conceivably in his late fifties, but more probably in his sixties. But people notoriously age at different rates, and so long as we realize that Strepsiades' mental and physical condition is such that he is regarded as an old man by himself and by others, his sum of years is irrelevant.

*Status.* Strepsiades lives 'far off in the country' (138). He is ignorant, stupid, and boorish, a son of the soil and smelling of the soil (43 ff.)—but one of its richer sons. He seems to have had no difficulty in borrowing, from people who knew him, very large sums of money, such as are not readily lent to farm-labourers or poor peasants. A distinguished aristocratic family sought him out (41 f.) as a husband for one of its daughters, and since this (to us) surprising marriage is taken for granted by Ar., without explanation or further comment, we should be justified in supposing that it did not surprise Ar.'s audience. In Menander's *Dyskolos* Knemon, a 'real Attic farmer' (604 ff.) owns land worth two talents (327 f.), i.e. about £12,000 in terms of modern purchasing power, and it is only his misanthropy that makes him try to cope with the work himself (163 f., 328 ff.) and live like a poor man (129 f.). Strepsiades, although he knows how to tighten his belt and has a farmer's mistrust of extravagance (421), is to be thought of as owning farm land which would nowadays sell for £60,000.

—Kenneth James Dover, *Clouds* (Oxford: Clarendon Press, 1968): pp. xxiii–xxv, xxvii–xxviii.

[Rosemary M. Harriott is the author of *Poetry and Criticism Before Plato* (1969). In the excerpt below from her chapter entitled "Clouds," Harriott discusses the relationship between Strepsiades-Pheidippides as a "comedy without a happy ending."]

The critical moment in *Clouds* occurs quite late in the play, when Strepsiades rushes out of his house to escape from his son, who has already punched his head and jaw (1321 f). From this moment Pheidippides demonstrates that he is superior to his father in argument as well as in physical strength and Strepsiades, seeing the results of his decisions and realising at last what he has brought upon himself, turns from optimism and confidence to bitterness and the desire for revenge. Thus the play ends, not with the usual merry-making that results from the hero's success, or at least creates a mood of jollity, but with a downturn. If this scene is critical in the shaping of the play, it is also crucial in another way, for it is here that the two elements, of rhetoric and family relationships, come together, or rather collide. In order to understand the nature and repercussions of the impact it may be helpful to trace each of the two elements separately up to this point, taking first the relationship which provides the mainspring of the plot. ⟨...⟩

Let me begin by looking at the traces of a simple and traditional comedy in which a sympathetic hero moves from anxiety to triumph. It is in fact to a play of this kind that our prologue actually seems to belong. Strepsiades' account of his problem and its causes serves to engage sympathy for himself and to encourage interest in the relationships within this family. The solution he proposes, that his son shall learn the art of successful speaking in order to evade his creditors, is presented in a way that discourages any question as to the morality of defaulting: sympathy for Strepsiades means sympathy for him as defendant in any suit to recover money owing. We seem to be going to watch a play in which private concerns will be paramount and in which the new rhetoric will be a useful tool for ordinary people to use, not something to be feared and deplored. ⟨...⟩

In composing a play of this kind, a comedy without a happy ending, the dramatist has adapted but reversed a pattern found in some tragedies at this period, a pattern which avoids complete and final disaster and permits the hero to escape from his troubles, at least for a time, while frustrating the hopes of his enemies. A tragedy which ends happily may well please the audience, if not the academic critics, but, when a comedy leaves its usual path in favour of one which leads to disappointment and unhappiness, contrary to the expectations of the spectators, there is the risk that the failure to provide a celebratory atmosphere at the end may lessen the chance of victory in the contest. On the other hand, there are advantages in avoiding the obvious and boring.

Clearly changing the pattern necessitates altering the normal comic structure since, to begin with the obvious factor, the play cannot end with scenes demonstrating the success of the hero's scheme. In fact the structural abnormalities of *Clouds* are quite considerable, and this can be shown by suggesting the form the 'simple' play might have taken and contrasting the result with our *Clouds*. If Strepsiades' plan had succeeded, the training in rhetoric would have been completed before the parabasis and the remainder of the play would have contained encounters with creditors followed by preparations for feasting. ⟨. . .⟩

—Rosemary M. Harriott, "Clouds," *Aristophanes: Poet and Dramatist* (Baltimore: The Johns Hopkins University Press, 1986): pp. 165–67.

## MARIE C. MARIANETTI ON POLITICAL SATIRE

[Marie C. Marianetti is the editor and translator of *The Clouds: An Annotated Translation* (1997). In the excerpt below from the chapter entitled "The Multifarious Clouds," Marianetti discusses the play as a political satire, focusing on the role of the chorus.]

Aristophanes' *Clouds* has been labeled a comedy of ideas rather than a comedy of political focus exploring the corruptions of the Athenian demagogy (apart from an isolated attack on Cleon in the parabasis 581ff.) and current matters of war and peace. It is, however, political in respect to its treatment of problems that have affected the stability of the polis in the confrontation of religious beliefs with imported ideas of a religious nature: the problems of pedagogy, the effects of rationalism upon morality, and the ⟨*nomos–physis*⟩ antitshesis as they are illustrated in the encounter between Strepsiades and Socrates, the contest between the two Logics and the generational conflict between father (Strepsiades) and son (Pheidippides). ⟨. . .⟩

The *Clouds* as a play may then best be described as a reflection of conflicting opposites, role reversals, character transformations, and double representations as regards the individual, natural (physical, environmental) and social domains; and the Clouds, as the representative chorus of the comic play, function as intermediaries between these conflicting opposites, in addition to embodying in themselves binary oppositions, role reversals and character transformation. ⟨. . .⟩

Chapter Three will discuss mainly sets of conflicting opposites. More specifically, it will inquire into the Cloud-chorus' transformational role in Aristophanes' *Clouds,* the opposing forces that it exposes and the chorus' reflection on the antithetical pairs of the play as a whole. It is this double exposition of the antithetical forces in the comic play which depicts more vividly the conflicting issues between novel ideas and conventional religious beliefs and practices. It is the transformational character of the Cloud-chorus which illustrates the confusion and contradiction that philosophical speculation, scepticism and science brought upon the uneducated, lower-class masses. And it is the antithetical pairs of the *Clouds* which correspond to the Pythagorean "table of opposites," that reveal Aristophanes' intention to caricature not only the impact of change upon traditional culture, but also the contradictory tendencies of the exponents of novelty themselves. This refers in particular to the inclination of the Pythagorean brotherhood to form separatist groups which stood apart and were different from the rest of the culture, and to the tendency of novel movements to attack the traditional past of a society which depended upon the glories of its past. Therefore, the role of the Cloud-chorus as intermediaries in the play will demonstrate the conflicting co-existence of the old and the new; and the transformation of the Cloud-chorus will exemplify the limitations of traditional culture and clarify social misunderstanding as regards the perception of novelty. ⟨. . .⟩

The divine appearance of the Cloud-chorus and its association with nature, then, depicts the Clouds as natural phenomena, dwellers of the free sky and the open air as well as beneficial to farming, crops and fields. It more or less reflects the conception of the clouds in the ordinary Greek mind as rain-bearing and thus benevolent. In addition, the divine attributes of the Cloud-chorus reinforce the Clouds' association with the praise of Attica, the land of Pallas and Cecrops, in the antistrophe. The chorus elaborates on the significance of the festivities, the dancing, the music, the sacrifices and the offering of gifts to the gods throughout the seasons— an encomium with special reference to the City Dionysia and the Eleusinian mysteries (since they constituted the most significant festivals of the Athenian polis, 299–313):

> —Marie C. Marianetti, "The Multifarious Clouds," *Religion and Politics in Aristophanes'* Clouds (Hildesheim: Zurich and New York: Olms-Weidmann, 1992): pp. 76–80.

## Daphne Elizabeth O'Regan on the Nature of Justice

[Daphne Elizabeth O'Regan is the author of *Rhetoric, Comedy, and the Violence of Language in Aristophanes'* Clouds (1992). In the excerpt below from the chapter entitled "Comic Justice: Lines 1303–1510," O'Regan discusses the nature of justice in the play as a comedy of inversion not to be confused with moral justice.]

The clouds' song at the end of the scene with the creditors (1303–20) warns the audience that the end of the play is at hand and hints at the form it will take. In the characteristic dynamic of the *Clouds*, we are about to witness the joke that will turn everything preceding on its head. Put in other terms, we will see comic justice at work, witnessing a "comedy of inversion," in which characters are entrapped by their desires and enmeshed in their own schemes. This process should not be confused with moral justice, although the effects may appear similar. Comic justice, like comic triumph, functions not morally but logistically. The end remains true to the strategy we have been studying all along: the creation of a metaphoric vision which operates by taking a *logos* "seriously," or "literally," rendering it concrete, and then drawing, or rather staging, the unexpected consequences. As the clouds indicate, this process is to begin with Strepsiades: this comic madman is going to find out what it is to "love" (*eran* 1303) the wrong things. Besotted (*erastheis* 1304) with the idea of denying his debts and the city's justice, he will feel the results of his desires: in the person of his son, Strepsiades, the "sophist" (1309–20), will experience what the *hetton logos* is really all about. However, the reversals will go further than that. Not just Strepsiades, but Pheidippides and Socrates too, will find themselves in the world designed by their desires and their *logoi*. The triumphant progress of rhetoric will be derailed as we discover the real meaning of the denial of binding obligations, the isolation of the sophist, the assimilation of language and violence, and life in the oven of the purely natural world. The only trouble is that the consequences, while ridiculous, are not happy. Nevertheless, we are not confronted with tragedy. The overly perfect and mocking symmetry of the end, coupled with delicate play with the audience's responses, continue to remind us that we are watching comic *logos*, not life, at work. The entire *Clouds* performs on a larger scale the function of the cloud chorus, mockery that reflects in appropriate (not identical) shapes the manias of its subjects—which are certainly not confined to Strepsiades but include Socrates, Pheidippides, and the Athenian public as well.

The pattern of the end begins to come clear when Strepsiades erupts from his house screaming for help (1321). After beating his unfortunate creditors, now he himself is beaten by a sophist, his own son. Apparently, Pheidippides, too, has learned the violent lesson implicit in sophistic martial imagery, a lesson so highly compatible with the disposition and desires of natural man. Accomplished speaker that he is, Pheidippides has deserted language. Why, and what this means, is suggested by the comic allusion placed at the beginning of the episode. As Strepsiades recounts the quarrels about the singing of traditional poets after dinner (1355ff.) that led up to his beating, Pheidippides interrupts indignantly: his father deserved a thrashing for bidding him sing "just as if [he were] entertaining cicadas" ⟨...⟩.

—Daphne Elizabeth O'Regan, "Comic Justice: Lines 1303–1510,"
*Rhetoric, Comedy, and the Violence of Language in Aristophanes'*
Clouds (New York and Oxford: Oxford University Press, 1992): pp.
114–15.

## STELLA P. REVARD ON PERCY BYSSHE SHELLEY'S POEM

[Stella P. Revard is the author of *Milton and the Tangles of
Neaera's Hair: The Making of the 1645 Poems* (1997) and *The
War in Heaven: Paradise Lost and the Tradition of Satan's
Rebellion* (1980). In the excerpt below from her article,
"Shelley and Aristophanes: "The Cloud" and *Clouds,*
269–290," Revard discusses some aspects of the play which
influenced Percy Bysshe Shelley's poem.]

In the summer of 1818 Shelley was observing with great delight the
clouds of the Italian sky and was reading with equal delight the
lyrical choruses of Aristophanes' play, *Clouds*. To the joining of these
two experiences we owe, I believe, the initial creative impulse for the
lyric poem, "The Cloud." ⟨. . .⟩

First of all, Aristophanes' Clouds speak, after a short introduction,
in the first person. They are goddesses of the upper air, queens of
thunder and lightning. They are pictured in the invocation inhab-
iting various abodes: the sacred snowy peaks of Olympus, the gar-
dens of Father Oceanus, the golden mouth of the Nile, where they
like girls stoop and dip their pitchers in the water. They are
described as ever-moving, ever-changing in shape and abode. As
they begin their song, it is both their dominance over Heaven and
Earth and their mutability which is stressed.

> Eternal Clouds,
> Let us arise and reveal ourselves,
> Dewy and bright,
> Moving from the depths of Father Oceanus
> To the wooded mountain height.
> 
> (*Clouds*, ll. 275–279)

These are eternal deities, solemn yet playful. With august eyes, they survey the entire earth: the harvest lands, rivers, oceans, which have been watered by their rain. Unlike the sun, who must always stay tirelessly in Heaven, the Clouds can move between Heaven and Earth. They can shake off their solemn deity, their deathless form, and as their mutability ordains appear as simple happy maidens singing in a chorus. And as the chorus draws near, it is precisely this change which Aristophanes records for us.

> Now from our deathless shape
> Let us shake the misty rain,
> And with an eye, far-seeing,
> Look on earth again.
>
> (Clouds, ll. 288–290)

Like Aristophanes' rain-goddesses, Shelley's cloud is "the daughter of Earth and Water / And the nursling of the Sky" (ll. (73–74). Wandering, she is led over the earth, piloted in her course by lightning. ⟨. . .⟩

As Aristophanes' clouds sit upon snowy Olympus or snow-capped Mimas, Shelley's cloud "sift[s] the snow on the mountains below" (l. 13). Or as they cover the tireless eye of Ether, she "bind[s] the Sun's throne with a burning zone, / And the Moon's with a girdle of pearl" (ll. 59–60). As they are goddesses over thunder and lightning and hail, she "wields[s] the flail of the lashing hail" (l. 9). Both poets stress the majesty of the clouds who from above survey the earth in a single glance. Aristophanes shows us the chorus of clouds looking down on the lovely vistas of nature—fertile fields, sparkling rivers, and oceans—as well as the crowded city with its processions and choral dances. Shelley has his lone cloud look only on the face of nature: the moist earth laughing below, the calm rivers, seas, and lakes in which the cloudy sky is mirrored (ll. 55–58).

Of course, Aristophanes' clouds are not only lyrical but comic presences, patronesses of fleecy-versed dithyrambic poets, mist-brained philosophers, those with their feet on the ground and their heads in the air. And Aristophanes makes much of the comic possibilities, likening the clouds to aerial stomachs full of gas and water which rumble with thunder and then burst forth with rain. Indeed, Aristophanes even has his clouds threaten that if they are not awarded first prize in the dramatic competition, they will drown the crops of Attica with rain and break the tiled roofs of the city with hail.

—Stella P. Revard, "Shelley and Aristophanes: "The Cloud" and *Clouds,* 269–290," *English Language Notes* 15, no. 3 (March 1978): pp. 188–91.

## Ian C. Storey on Attitudes Towards the Sophists

[Ian C. Storey has written the Introduction to Peter Mei-neck's translation of *Clouds.* In the excerpt below from that introduction, Storey discusses the conflicting perspectives in Aristophanes' satire on the sophistic teachers.]

*Clouds* is certainly Aristophanes best-known comedy. If modern readers know one of his plays, it is usually this one, although in the late years of the twentieth century, *Lysistrata* may run a close second. The manuscript tradition and the accompanying scholia are by far the fullest for *Clouds,* and the anecdotal tradition in ancient authors concerning this play is equally large. This is of course due to the presence of the august (dare one say "saintly"?) figure of Socrates in the comedy. Plato and Xenophon created a character of legendary importance in classical culture, and Aristophanes' contemporary caricature of him attracted a huge amount of attention.

The play revolves around an old country farmer, Strepsiades ("Twister"), whose son, Pheidippides, has run him deeply into debt through an upper-class lifestyle and a passion for horses. His "great idea": for his son to enter the *phrontisterion* ("Pondertorium") of Socrates where he will learn the Inferior Argument, which "can debate an unjust case and win" (115), and thus talk his way out of his father's debts. When the son refuses to obey, Strepsiades goes himself to learn from Socrates. ⟨. . .⟩

Whitman argued that Aristophanic comedy featured a recurring type of comic hero, the old countryman who achieves his great idea and comes out on top through a streak of *poneria* ("knavery," "roguishness") at the heart of his personality, and Strepsiades certainly fits this model. Much is made in the prologue of his country roots and attitudes, as opposed to the luxury (decadence?) of the town, and while he may lack the grandiose imagination of Dicaeopolis (*Acharnians*) or Peithetaerus (*Birds*), the earnestness of Trygaeus (*Peace*) or Lysistrata, or the irrepressibility of Procleon (*Wasps*), he does possess a down-to-earth cunning, a simplicity that the spectator will find appealing. Simply put, he is the ideal sort to "take the piss" out of sophistic pretensions. The teaching scene (627–804) shows Aristophanes at his comic best where the less-than-bright Strepsiades foils every attempt by Socrates to teach him anything. Yet the scene depends on stretching the spectator's reactions in two opposite directions: he wants to be a *sophos* like Socrates, for (unlike Strepsiades) he knows about measures and rhythms, and at the same time wants to see the *sophos* taken down a rung or two. We admire Strepsiades' low cunning and desire not to pay his debts, but at the same time we wince at his essential dishonesty and insistence at learning the Inferior Argument. It can be observed that the "great idea" is undone at the end, that Strepsiades repents of what he has done (1462–4), that the play ends with destruction rather than jubilation or reconciliation. But the ending is one place that we know was altered in the revision, and the original may well have ended differently.

*Clouds* may be less "political" than other plays of the 420s—if it were not for the passing reference at line 7, we would not know that Athens was at war at this time—but it is no less topical. *Clouds* dramatizes a contact with what we call the "Enlightenment," the intellectual fervor that burst on the Greeks in the fifth century. Beginning with the Ionian physical scientists of the sixth century, it went far beyond inquiries on the physical nature of the universe; the thinkers of the fifth century raised the great questions of ethics, being, political science, anthropology, language, and even of the nature of knowledge itself.

—Ian C. Storey, *Clouds,* trans. with notes by Peter Meineck (Indianapolis and Cambridge: Hackett Publishing Company, Inc., 2000): pp. xxxv–xxxvii.

# Plot Summary of
## *The Frogs*

*The Frogs* (*Batrachoi*) was produced at the Lenaia in January of 405 B.C. and won first prize. The Athenians had been at war almost the entire time since 431 B.C. and their situation at this time was almost desperate. It was written during the end of the Peloponnesian War when Athens was tired of war and suffering from political chaos. Aristophanes' play is skillful blending of literary and political satire, suggesting the need for an ethical and inspired poet, one who would dramatize the superior characteristics of a hero, a courageous man larger than life, who would fulfill his responsibilities. In *The Frogs*, Aristophanes is calling out for a dramatist who could bring back traditional values and virtue to the citizens of Athens.

The basic plot of *The Frogs* is that of a quest and the accompanying trials and tests that the protagonist, Dionysus, must experience in pursuit of his goal. Nevertheless, *The Frogs* is a comedy and not an epic tale of heroic feats and brave acts such as to be found in Homer's *Odyssey* and *Iliad*. In its simplest terms, the story is about the god Dionysus journeying to Hades to bring back the now deceased dramatist, Euripides, because Athens is in "need of a poet who can write." Dionysus states that the only poets nowadays are "the slick and the dead." Dionysus is the god of the vineyards, wine and dramatic poetry and associated with poetic inspiration. However, in *The Frogs*, Dionysus is shorn of his divine powers and arrives in the underworld with his slave, Xanthias, where he soon learns that he must be the arbiter of a vituperative debate between two tragedians, Euripides and Aeschylus. Euripides was the Athenian tragedian (480–406 B.C.) whose character and plays were consistently ridiculed by Aristophanes for his realistic treatment of men as they are and the human psychology of their personalities, while Aeschylus, is depicted as a traditional Athenian playwright (525–456 B.C.), whose tragedies are based on a build up of tension and expectation towards an anticipated climax by his audience. In the ensuing contest, Dionysus is forced to become a judge in which the two playwrights are competing for the throne in Hades. In the end, contrary to his initial intention, Dionysus declares Aeschylus the winner and brings him back to earth.

The opening scene of **Act One** takes place on the outskirts of Athens, with Dionysus and his servant, Xanthias, just outside the house of Heracles, the hero and demigod renowned for his great labors and prodigious strength. Dionysus is here wearing a yellow tunic appropriate to a Dionysiac celebration and the buskins or high-laced boots traditionally associated with tragedy, while at the same time imitating Heracles' attire of lion's skin and carrying a club. Xanthias is sitting atop a donkey, relentlessly complaining about the weight of Dionysus' baggage which he carries on a pole. The two are on their way to see Heracles, the greatest of Greek heroes, endowed with both human and divine attributes, adopted by both individuals and the state as a symbol of a protecting deity, presiding over warfare and military training. When Heracles answers their knock upon his door, he responds hilariously to the absurd aspect of Dionysus, wearing "a lion-skin over a yellow nightdress." Dionysus quickly explains that he is on a mission to find the recently-deceased Euripides in the underworld and he is seeking Heracles' advice because Heracles' had once made the voyage to Hades. The questions Dionysus poses to Heracles are those of a prospective tourist familiarizing himself with the fastest route to his destination and most commodious accommodations to be found upon his arrival. "I wondered if perhaps you could give me a few tips: any useful contacts down there, where you get the boat, which are the best eating-houses, bread shops, wine shops, knocking shops . . . And which places have the fewest bugs." After joking with Dionysus about committing suicide as a sure route to Hades, "[y]ou could go via Rope and Gibbet: that's a very quick way, if you don't mind hanging around for a bit to begin with," Heracles describes the horrific conditions there. "And then you come to the Great Muck Marsh and the Eternal River of Dung—you'll find some pretty unsavoury characters floundering about in that." Nevertheless, Dionysus refuses to be deterred or frightened.

When Dionysus finally arrives at the River Styx, Charon refuses to transport Xanthias because he is a slave who has not compensated for this lowly status by engaging in a sea battle. Although Xanthias quickly explains that he was exempted for medical reasons, he is forced to navigate the perimeter of the river on foot, while Dionysus, in another example of endless insults to his divine status, is made to pick up the oars and row himself. Charon is extremely rude to the god, referring to Dionysus as a "pot-bellied loon." He does this to the hilarious accompaniment of an invisible chorus of frogs singing their famous refrain, "Brekekekex, ko-ax, ko-ax." Furthermore, when Dionysus asks the frogs to stop, "my melodious friends, put a sock on it, can't you?," the frogs sing even louder forcing Dionysus to join in on the refrain.

In the next scene, having arrived in Hades, Dionysus gazes upon the murderers and perjurers of whom he was warned and, when he and Xanthias hear a flute, they hide as the torch-bearing Chorus of Men and Women enter with their respective Leaders. They praise Dionysus and entreat him to participate in their rites, while asking the profane to leave. "We've no use for bounders who don't under-stand / The traditions of Comedy noble and grand; / Who snigger and leer till the festival's ended, / And find dirty meanings where none are intended." It is important to note that those who are deemed unworthy of participating are the politicians who accept bribes, "[t]he greedy official who's even prepared / [t]o betray his own City, if suitably squared" and the Athenians who attempt to censor the writers of comedy. "Some people there are who, when guyed in a play, / Take it out on the poet by cutting his pay." Soon Dionysus and Xanthias join the chorus, with Dionysus asking the chorus for directions to Pluto's home.

The next scene finds Dionysus and Xanthias before the palace of Pluto, wondering in what manner they should knock on the door. Once they arrive, they are greeted by Aeacus, the very rude and insulting doorkeeper to the entrance of Hades, who threatens to throw both of them "down to the black-hearted Stygian rocks" where they will be pursued by "the prowling hounds of Hell and the hundred-headed viper." Sufficiently frightened, Dionysus asks Xan-thias to exchange clothes, only to regret it shortly thereafter as the maid of Persephone greets Xanthias, inviting him to a feast replete with a curious group of dancing girls. "Hand-plucked, and all in the freshest bloom of middle age." However, as soon as Dionysus again assumes the attire of Herkales, he encounters a landlady who scolds him for not having paid his bill. It is interesting to note that the exchange of identities and experiences between master and servant is characteristic of Old Comedy where the normal social order of the world is turned upside down, a reversal made even more emphatic as Dionysus was a prominent god in Greek mythology.

Shortly thereafter, as a result of his encounter with a disgruntled landlady, who accuses the god of being the "scoundrel who came to our inn once and ate up sixteen loaves," Dionysus is arrested by some slaves, which is to say that Xanthias becomes the culprit for he has once again changed disguises with his master. Indeed, the arrest is made with Dionysus suggesting that they torture his servant. This would be in accordance with Athenian custom, as a slave could be forced to testify against his master and is a prime example of Aristophanes' political satire on the dangerous situation in Athens. Needless to say that when Dionysus reveals his true divine identity within this very absurd context of shifting identities, Aeacus refuses to believe him. Both Dionysus and Xanthias are to be beaten on the assumption that a true god will not experience pain or suffering, but when they both cry out, they must be brought before those who will be able to recognize a god. "I'm blest if I can tell which of you is the god. You'll have to come inside. The master and Persephone'll be able to tell all right: they're gods themselves."

After they leave, the chorus sings the parabasis, in which it attacks the demagogue Cleophon for objecting to make peace with Sparta during the last terrible years of the Peloponnesian War. The chorus pleads that the oligarchs who seized power in 411 B.C., and who have since been sent into exile, be returned to Athens. "And first for those misguided souls I plead / Who in the past to Phrynichus paid heed. 'Tis history now—their folly they regret; / The time has come to pardon and forget." The Chorus maintains that the old and respected families should be valued over the newcomers.

**Act Two** takes place before Pluto's palace with Xanthias and Aeacus engaged in light housekeeping chores. Aeacus is praising Xanthias for his disrespect towards Dionysus. "Why, there's nothing I like better than cursing the master behind his back." But this banter is interrupted by the sounds of people arguing and, as it turns out, the combatants are the dead dramatists, Aeschylus and Euripides, quarreling about which one has the right to dine at the table of Hades. As it turns out, Aeschylus preceded Euripides in this place of honor until Euripides usurped this privilege. It has been decided that a competition must take place between the two playrights, their poetry to be weighed line by line with Dionysus presiding as the judge. But, before the games begin, each playwright prays to his gods —Aeschylus praying to Demeter, goddess of the corn, and Euripides praying to his own gods: Ether, his vocal cords, reason and his sense of smell.

Aeschylus accuses Euripides of pandering to the tastes of thieves and other disreputable denizens of the Underworld. "And what are your tragedies but a concatenation of commonplaces, as threadbare as the tattered characters who utter them?" In rebuttal, Euripides counters by accusing his opponent of being "a mountebank and an imposter," of using "words that made you dizzy to hear them." Each one defends his own style and subject matter. Euripides boasts of his simplicity and use of material from everyday life in direct opposition to Aeschylus' style. "When I took over Tragedy from you, the poor creature was in a desperate state. Fatty degeneration of the Art. All swollen up with high-falutin diction." For his defense, Aeschylus maintains that Euripides's realism is immoral. "My heroes weren't like these market-place loafers, swindlers and rogues they write about nowadays: they were real heroes, breathing spears and lances." Though Dionysus finds it hard to decide the winner, and although both dramatists are his friends, he ultimately decides to bring the traditional and conservative Aeschylus back to Athens as the poet most capable of redeeming Athens. And in this he has the approval of the Chorus. "So altogether we're glad to find / That a man with a shrewd and intelligent mind / (A man with a sense of proportion) / . . . Is returning to Earth, in this decadent age / To save the city and save the stage / From politics, lies and distortion." ✿

# List of Characters in
## *The Frogs*

**Dionysus**

**Xanthias,** his slave

**Heracles**

**Corpse**

**Charon:** ferryman of the souls of the dead across the River Styx

**Chorus:** as Frogs, as Initiates, and as the population of Hades

**Aeacus:** the doorkeeper of Hades

**Maid:** to Persephone

**Two Landladies**

**An Elderly Slave:** servant to Pluto

**Euripides:** a dramatist

**Aeschylus:** a dramatist

**Pluto:** god of the Underworld

**A Castanet Girl**

**Corpse-Bearers, Slaves, Dancing Girls, Distinguished Residents of Hades** ❀

# Critical Views on
## *The Frogs*

PETER ARNOTT ON THE PLAY AS METACRITICISM

[Peter Arnott is the author of *An Introduction to French Theater* (1977) and "Greek Drama and the Modern Stage" (1964). In the excerpt below from his article, "Aristophanes and Popular Comedy: An Analysis of *The Frogs*," Arnott discusses the play as metacriticism of plays and playwrights, focusing here on Dionysus.]

As the study of popular theatre tends to concern itself with nonliterary or subliterary forms, it may seem curious that I have chosen to present, in this connection, the detailed scrutiny of a literary text. I do so in the conviction that, in Aristophanes, traditional scholarly and editorial analysis has often failed to provide a satisfactory solution to crucial problems; and that such problems may well respond to a more pragmatic type of analysis based on modes of performance rather than on literary genres. The Aristophanic *vis comica* is hard to define, harder to translate, and harder still to reproduce on the modern stage. Nevertheless, if we can say anything with conviction about Aristophanes, it is this: that his work was firmly grounded in a tradition of popular farce that he acknowledges, implicitly or explicitly, in virtually every page that he writes. It has been my good fortune to be involved in the production and performance of Aristophanes perhaps more often than most; and I hope, in this paper, by using one controversial scene as a test case, to show how the examination of traditional comic devices, which are essentially those of the popular theatre, may illuminate the interpretation of a passage which has defied conventional exegesis.

The year 405 BC was not a happy one for Athens. The war with Sparta was nearly lost; racked by internal dissension and driven into desperate courses by mismanagement, the city seemed to delight in inflicting on itself the wounds it was unable to inflict on others. Yet one event at least helped to lighten the beginning of this dismal year. At the Festival of the Lenaea, Aristophanes presented his comedy *The Frogs*. It was, unlike some of his earlier plays, a complete and immediate success, and was rewarded with the unique tribute of a repeat performance. In our own time, though less popular on the stage, it has won distinction of a different and less satisfactory sort. Perhaps no comedy, out of the eleven by Aristophanes which have survived, has been more keenly scrutinised for hidden meanings and recondite allusion; perhaps no comedy of any author has laboured under so heavy a burden of irrelevant scholarship.

*The Frogs* is a play about plays and playwrights, tragedy and trage-dians. Its action concerns the journey of the God of Tragedy, Dionysus, to the Underworld, with the purpose of resurrecting the poet Euripides, who had died shortly before the play was produced. Thus, argues Dionysus, the tragic stage will be restored to its old glory and his own worship preserved. In the second half of the comedy, Aristophanes allows Dionysus, without explanation, to depart from his declared intention. Once he has arrived in Hades, he does not simply take Euripides back to earth. Rather, he presides over a debate between that poet and his illustrious predecessor Aeschylus, announcing that whoever wins the contest shall be his first choice. Whether or not it was this section of the play that most pleased the ancient audience, it has certainly been the principal delight of modern scholars, and one scene in particular has been turned into an angrily contested tilting ground where many a critical lance has been shattered, not only in the name of Aristophanes but on behalf of Aeschylus and Euripides also.

I refer, of course, to the famous 'oil-flask' scene. After sweeping condemnations have been uttered on both sides, the tragedians turn to attacking each other's work piecemeal. Euripides has just assailed Aeschylus' prologues on the grounds of obscurity, arguing that they are repetitious and confused. Aeschylus now retaliates by forcing Euripides to quote a number of examples from his own prologues. He reduces each in turn to absurdity by interrupting just before the end, and substituting for the proper words the tag 'and lost his oil-flask' (*lekythion apolesen*).

—Peter Arnott, "Aristophanes and Popular Comedy: An Analysis of *The Frogs*," *Western Popular Theatre,* ed. David Mayer and Kenneth Richards (London and New York: Methuen & Co., 1977): pp. 169–70.

[David Barrett is a translator (with Alan Sommerstein) of the Penguin edition of Aristophanes' *The Knights, Peace, The Birds, The Assemblywomen and Wealth* (1978). In the excerpt below from his introduction to *The Wasps, The Poet and The Women and The Frogs,* Barrett hypothesizes on some staging details in the opening scenes.]

Assuming the stage arrangements to have been roughly as I have described them (though it must be repeated that many details are matters of conjecture), it is interesting to work out the way in which some of the scenes in the comedies must have been staged, and see how Aristophanes exploited his resources. Often there are cues in the text to help us. Let us take a look, for example, at the opening scenes of *The Frogs*.

Dionysus, puffing and panting, and Xanthias, on his human donkey, enter the *orchestra* by the *parodos,* passing close to a section of the audience, whom Xanthias surveys with disgust. As they mount the steps to the stage, and the conversation turns upon burdens, attention is called to the plight of the 'donkey': 'you'd better change places with him', Dionysus suggests. At last they reach the stage proper, and the door of Heracles' house. ('You see, I've walked the whole way.') Dionysus and Heracles converse, while Xanthias and his mount provide comic business in the background. Eventually the donkey wanders off, via the *parodos,* and re-enters the stage building from the rear. Heracles says good-bye to Dionysus, whips off his mask and lion-skin, lies down on a stretcher, and is carried out of another door as the Corpse. (The ex-donkey is now one of the bearers.) After being intercepted by Dionysus, the Corpse is carried down the steps (this would suggest a descent to the underworld) and out by the *parodos.* As soon as he is out of sight, the Corpse nips through the back door into the dressing-room, and a moment later returns as Charon, poling his comical boat-on-wheels along the *parodos* towards the *orchestra*. Dionysus and Xanthias, who have had to carry out a bit of business with the luggage to give time for all this, now start their downward journey. By this time Charon, already visible to most of the audience, is just rounding the corner of the stage: Dionysus and Xanthias see the prow of the boat before Charon himself comes into view. They descend to the 'shore': Dionysus gets into the boat, but Xanthias is told that he will have to walk right round the 'lake', i.e. the *orchestra*. This he does, probably by a roundabout route, frequently losing his way among the gangways of the auditorium. Meanwhile the boat is launched, and Dionysus rows right out into the 'open waters' of the *orchestra*. The Frogs now enter, leaping and hopping, by the *parodos* (greeted, perhaps, by a cheer from the audience, who think they are the real Chorus: after all, the title of the play has been announced as *The Frogs*). They dance around the boat, singing and croaking in chorus, until Dionysus succeeds in driving them away. By this time he has rowed right across to the side of the *orchestra* farthest from the stage, and he lands at the feet of his own priest in the centre of the front row of seats. Charon rows rapidly away, and Xanthias rejoins his master. But now the Empusa appears, a fearsome monster which keeps changing its shape: perhaps some of the frog-dancers again, in horrific masks, peeping out in turn from under a blanket. Dionysus, in terror, clutches the skirts of his priest, and then flees up the central gangway, to the delight of the audience. But Xanthias suceeds in exorcising the apparition. They start back towards the stage, but now the real Chorus enters, and they are obliged to crouch down at the edge of the *orchestra,* where they remain until they decide to join in the dancing themselves. The dance brings them back to the foot of the stage steps, and when Dionysus inquires the way to the palace, the Chorus reply 'It's just behind you now'—and so, by Pluto, it is. They have reached their journey's end.

—David Barrett, *The Wasps, The Poet and The Women and The Frogs* (London and New York: The Penguin Group, 1964): pp. 23–24.

MAURICE CROISET ON THE IMPORTANCE OF AESCHYLUS

[Maurice Croiset is the author of *An Abridged History of Greek Literature* (1970) and *Hellenic Civilization: An Historical Survey* (1925). In the excerpt below from his chapter entitled, "The Sicilian and Deceleian Wars," Croiset discusses Artistophanes' moral preference for Aeschylus over Euripides.]

Was there any change in Aristophanes' political views between the years 411 and 405, between the *Thesmophoriazusae* and the *Frogs*? The only document by which we are able to judge of this is the comedy of the *Frogs* itself, performed at the Lenaea under the Archon Callias, toward the end of January, 405. ⟨. . .⟩

Outside of Athens everything was slowly tending toward the final catastrophe. Athenian successes at sea, though they were sometimes brilliant and unexpected, were not followed up, because there no longer existed either the firmness of will or the resources necessary to continue them. ⟨. . .⟩ And yet the Athenian democracy, under the influence of Cleophon, was more intractable than ever. It had rejected the overtures of peace which Sparta had made after the battle of Arginusae, and, not satisfied with sacrificing the victorious generals to a fanatical superstition which certain politicians basely stirred up, it made itself odious by the inhuman measures which it decreed against those of the enemy who had been taken as prisoners.

It is at this juncture, in the autumn of 406, that Aristophanes must have written his *Frogs*. ⟨. . .⟩

It is not to be denied that the *Frogs* contains bitter personal attacks on the demagogues; the play, indeed, as a whole, has a satirical tone that must not be ignored. But these personal attacks are scattered—they are shafts hurled in passing, and the satire in general is aimed at the moral condition of the entire city and not at its leaders or advisers. ⟨. . .⟩

He no longer attacks even institutions or their abuses, as he had formerly done in the *Knights* or in the *Wasps*. At most, we might call attention to a sharp word about the "two obols," and this is more of a joke than of a criticism (l. 141). This is a mere detail, without consequence. The underlying intention of the play is of quite a different nature.

It appears chiefly in the comparison between Aeschylus and Euripides, which forms the subject of the play. As we know, this comparison, which is entirely to the disadvantage of Euripides, is at the same time literary and moral; but the moral part seems to be of greater consequence to the poet than the literary, and precisely herein lies the novelty of his point of view. For a very long time he had shown himself an emphatic opponent of Euripides; he had already made fun of him in the *Acharnians*, the earliest of his extant comedies. He continued to make fun of him in the *Clouds,* the *Peace,* and in the *Thesmophoriazusae,* to say nothing of the plays that have been lost. In all this ridicule it was especially Euripides' art, his dramatic effects that were made fun of. His moral influence was referred to only incidentally. Here, quite the contrary is the case. From the point of view of art, the comedy might make us hesitate between the two poets. Although Aristophanes appears to prefer Aeschylus, he is not above making his audience laugh at his archaic style and his obscure grandiloquence. On the other hand, again, even though he ridicules certain of Euripides' methods, he shows, by the utterances of Dionysus, that he recognizes the fascination he had for people. But so far as moral influence is concerned, the comparison is as decidedly as possible in favor of Aeschylus. If we listen to the comic poet, it would almost seem as if the victories of the Persian wars had been of his making, whereas the mournful state of Athenian affairs in 405 must be laid at Euripides' door.

> —Maurice Croiset, "The Sicilian and Deceleian Wars," *Aristophanes and the Political Parties at Athens* (London: Macmillan and Co., Limited, 1909): pp. 147–51.

## JOSEPH A. DANE ON THE LITERARY FUNCTION OF EURIPIDES

[Joseph A. Dane is the author of "Parody, Satire and Genre in The Tournament of Tottenham (1400–1440)" (1997) and *Who Is Buried in Chaucer's Tomb?: Studies in the Reception of Chaucer's Book* (1998). In the excerpt below from the chapter entitled "Aristophanes' Euripides 3: From Performance to Text (*The Frogs* and *The Clouds*)," Dane discusses the literary function of Euripides in *The Frogs* and the transformation of play into text.]

As in *The Acharnians* and in *Thesmophoriazusae,* Euripides is a central character in *The Frogs.* But the Euripides of *The Frogs* is not the Euripides of Aristophanes' earlier plays. He is less a dramatic machinator than a composer of literary texts. And the parody Aristophanes directs against him is a form of literary criticism. Aristophanes has often been regarded as one of the first literary critics, and Aristophanes becomes a literary critic in the transformation between part 1 and part 2 of *The Frogs*. Here drama ceases to be defined by the *bomolokhos* Dionysos and his slave Xanthias and becomes defined by two verbal artists, Euripides and Aeschylus.

Fifth-century plays were generally intended for a single performance in an Athenian theater. All subsequent performances are "revivals," "revisions," "museum pieces," and all are based on texts which exist independently of the original performance. A "version" of a play could be put on outside Athens. In *The Republic* 475b, Plato speaks of the theatergoer who would miss none of the plays at the Dionysia or in the country, and we can assume that some of the plays performed in the rural festivals were the plays performed in Athens. Plays were also revived in the fourth century, under different playing conditions. And these later performances may be responsible for the notes on production contained in the scholia, notes on which many of our conjectures regarding fifth-century modes of production are based. But even as I write here, the meaning of the word "play" is changing—it no longer means "action"; it refers instead to an archetypal text (a virtual text) that is abstracted from all these versions. ⟨. . .⟩

In *The Frogs*, Aristophanes sets up a distinction between the living production and the archaic text. The victory goes to the text; Aeschylus's words outlive his drama. The same conclusion is attained in *The Clouds*. Whatever the changes introduced by Aristophanes, he has succeeded in creating a text, a literary document—a status his other plays attain only through history. To do this, he used the very conventions that distinguish Old Comedy generically. The chorus assumes multiple roles in Old Comedy, and here it assumes an impossible role: it speaks of the living production as a matter of history. The chorus objectifies the work as past history and present text. This is Aristophanes' final revenge on his audience. In *The Frogs* he creates a parodic mode of criticism from which his own work is immune (his attack is confined to tragic texts). Here he redefines comedy as text. His theatrical audience, a crowd of spectators, ceases to exist; it vanishes before the literary audience—the "most wise" who can read his text.

A distinguishing mark of Old Comedy was its parodic disdain of the very conventions through which it is intelligible and its satiric disdain of the society which enabled it to exist. According to Platonius, the satiric freedom enjoyed by Old Comedy led to reprisals and to its suppression: Old Comedy playwrights were afraid; chorus leaders could not be found. Platonius is concerned with the attacks of Old Comedy on society, but his argument could also include the attacks of Old Comedy on itself. What leads to a transformation of Old Comedy into Middle and New Comedy is its self-parody—the challenging and refuting of the very dramatic conventions on which it was based. The production of parody led to the production of literature. And a drama reduced to literature is no longer drama at all.

—Joseph A. Dane, "Aristophanes' Euripides 3: From Performance to Text (*The Frogs* and *The Clouds*)," *Parody: Critical Concepts versus Literary Practices, Aristophanes to Sterne* (Norman and London: University of Oklahoma Press, 1988): pp. 48–49 and 63–64.

## THOMAS K. HUBBARD ON *THE FROGS* IN GREEK LITERATURE

[Thomas K. Hubbard is the author of *The Pipes of Pan: Intertextuality and Literary Filation in the Pastoral Tradition from Theocritus to Milton* (1998) and *The Pindaric Mind: A Study of Logical Structure in Early Greek Poetry* (1985). In the chapter entitled "From Birds to Frogs," Hubbard discusses *The Frogs* in terms of its place in the history of Greek literature.]

Because the *Frogs* is not only our last surviving work of Old Comedy but is itself concerned with the decline both of Athenian drama and political greatness, it occupies a special place in the history of Greek literature. Even more than Euripides' *Bacchae* or Sophocles' *Oedipus at Colonus,* the *Frogs* stands as a retrospection on an era coming to a close, in both literature and politics. Aristophanes' chief prototype for the idea of a descent to Hades to retrieve great figures of the past who could assist Athens in its present difficulties was Eupolis' *Demoi,* which brought back to life Solon, Miltiades, Aristides, and Pericles. Aristophanes makes the significant shift of bringing back to

Athens a tragic poet, not a statesman, in order to reflect the recent deaths of Sophocles and Euripides. But the *Frogs* is from beginning to end imbued with political as well as poetic themes, and Dionysus' final choice of Aeschylus seems to be determined more by political symbolism than by aesthetic superiority. The play's choruses and parabasis perform a pivotal role in coordinating its political and literary dimensions.

In the *Frogs* we also discover a generic concern about Comedy itself, a matter mostly absent in *Birds, Lysistrata,* and *Thesmophoriazusae,* but quite important in Aristophanes' earlier plays, as we have seen. Segal has discussed the development of Dionysus within the play as the god of Comedy who progressively assumes his role after much self-doubt and many changes of identity. In this respect he resembles some of Aristophanes' earlier protagonists, such as Dicaeopolis, the Sausage seller, Bdelycleon, or Trygaeus, who emerge as symbolic figures for Aristophanic Comedy, in their different ways combining lofty ambitions with earthy means of accomplishment. Dionysus' character expresses the same duality and ambivalence, oscillating as it does between bravado and effeminate cowardice, between the heroic costume of the great Heracles and the mundane garments of a slave.

The overall movement of the play progresses from a farcical first half with a weak and uncertain Dionysus to a more serious second half, in which Dionysus assumes the role of judge and mediator. Critics have on occasion been troubled by the *Frogs'* atypical structure, with the major agon coming after the parabasis and the series of farcical genre scenes coming before; they have also had difficulty in discerning any clear connection between the thematics of Dionysus' journey in the first half and the tragic contest in the second half of the play. Aristophanes may have structured the play as he did precisely to make a point about the relation of the comic and serious (as the chorus puts it in vv. 391–92, "saying many funny things and many serious things") and the necessity of approaching the serious through the comic. It has been observed that the part of the play before the parabasis features all the well-worn comic topoi Aristophanes abjures elsewhere: the glutton Heracles (vv. 503–73), slave beating (vv. 610–73), primitive animal choruses (vv. 207–68). The slave Xanthias opens the play by asking Dionysus whether he should say "one of the customary things the spectators always laugh at" (vv. 1–2) and Dionysus consents, prohibiting only the use of certain grossly physical terms and jokes that are nevertheless used in the very act of banning them, and indirectly, later on (see vv. 479–91). The simultaneous disavowal and use of these clichés foreshadow the slapstick technique of the section as a whole. As in so many other cases Aristophanes ironically announces his disdain for the very devices he employs, thus profiting from their theatrical value and at the same time appearing to be above them.

—Thomas K. Hubbard, "From Birds to Frogs," *The Mask of Comedy: Aristophanes and the Intertextual Parabasis* (Ithaca and London: Cornell University Press, 1991): pp. 199–201.

## ISMENE LADA-RICHARDS ON THE CULT OF DIONYSUS

[In the excerpt below from her chapter entitled "'Dionysiac' and 'Heraclean' in the Prologue of the *Frogs*," Ismene Lada-Richards discusses the relevance of the cult of Dionysus within the play.]

The first word belongs to Dionysus, the formidable, multifaceted god, who fired the imagination of poets and artists throughout antiquity and beyond, the ambiguous god, who, despite having sparked 'a wider spectrum of different and often contradictory interpretations' (Henrichs 1984*a*: 240) than any other Greek divinity, still remains as 'elusive' and defying definition (cf. Henrichs 1984*a*: 209), as mysterious and surprising as ever. 〈. . .〉

〈. . .〉 The problem arises from the fact that, to date, interpreters of Aristophanes have confined themselves to a *purely theatrical* appreciation of this god as a stock dramatic character, a mere generic type. In essence, not much has changed since Cornford's (1914: 238) schematic categorization of Dionysus in the *Frogs* as a 'Buffoon'; although few scholars now venture one-sided characterizations of Dionysus, Dover's (1993: 40–1) conclusion

> So in *Frogs* the comic Dionysos is treated in isolation from the multifarious legends, cults, and functions of which a divine person, called in all cases 'Dionysos', was the nucleus

is the result of a similar overall restriction of viewpoint and perspective. My book, instead, starts primarily from the assumption that spectators going to the theatre *cannot* and *do not* leave at home the whole framework of more general cultural, ideological, ethical principles which they apply to their extra-theatrical activities (Elam 1980: 52), and that, for this very reason, a 'stage-Dionysus' cannot be separated from the range of aspects, levels of meaning, and functions which were attached to his mythic, ritual, and cultic counterpart. This is particularly true not only for fifth-century Athens, where a dramatic festival, whether the City Dionysia or the Lenaea, is an inherent, organic part of the city's religious, social, cultural, and political life, but also for any classical Greek community, as an ancient god's divine 'personality' is not a fixed and static concept, but flexible, raw, mouldable material, with great capacities of adaptation, transformation, and assimilation. ⟨. . .⟩ In other words, as there is a constant interaction between cultural context and stage drama, we cannot hope to understand the dramatic hero of the *Frogs* without first attempting to understand what his real-life counterpart, the Dionysus of the *polis'* religious tradition, meant for his original spectators, the Aristophanic audience of late fifth-century Athens. And, as our view of the play in its entirety is bound to be conditioned by our interpretation of its protagonist, this book aims to fill a gap in the scholarship of Old Athenian Comedy by offering a reading of *Frogs* while primarily focusing on the central role and function of Dionysus in it. ⟨. . .⟩

An account of Dionysus' cult in the classical Athenian city obviously falls outside the scope of this study. Let it suffice to highlight at this point the main Dionysiac areas that we shall deal with in the chapters to follow, that is, wine, maenadism, theatre, and the afterlife.

Being men's 'companion in festivity' at *symposia* and drunken revelries alike; poured out to the rest of the Olympians at libations in every feast and festival of a *polis'* sacred calendar; being the prototype of a stage-actor's dramatic transformations and the divine model for his experience of 'getting out' of himself; driving women to 'ritual madness' and binding them together in a feeling of 'communion' with his *thiasos;* finally, 'liberating', as Dionysus Lysios, the initiate in his mysteries from the fear of death, and promising to him or her a blissful afterlife, Dionysus is everywhere, an essential part of the everyday life, experience, and activities of the Athenian classical spectator. Furthermore, being the god who has left the most overwhelming and most wide-ranging record of evidence in the ancient world, Dionysus is firmly fixed in the cultural 'encyclopaedia' of every Greek spectator. And it cannot be emphasized too strongly that it is precisely *through this 'encyclopaedia'* which accompanied, as it were, the audience into the theatre, that Dionysiac plays were viewed and mentally processed.

—Ismene Lada-Richards, "'Dionysiac' and 'Heraclean' in the Prologue of the Frogs," *Initiating Dionysus: Ritual and Theatre in Aristophanes' Frogs* (Oxford and New York: Clarendon Press, 1999): pp. 1–3.

# Plot Summary of
## *Lysistrata*

An Old Comedy performed in 411 B.C. by Aristophanes. By the time this play was performed, Athens had already endured serious defeats in the Peloponnesian War with Sparta and was thus incapable of achieving peace while saving face. Many Athenians had been killed in the Sicilian Expedition of 413 B.C. and the morale of the people was quite low. Some of Athens' strongest allies had turned against her. And, whereas in earlier plays such as *The Acharnians* and *Peace* we find Aristophanes arguing for a peaceful resolution with Sparta, when it was still a real possibility, in *Lysistrata*, he is expressing his yearning for the end of Athenian suffering and for a happy unification of the Greek states. And here the yearning for peace is done through the vehicle of a witty fantasy.

**The opening scene** takes place in Athens. On one side is the house of Lysistrata, and on the other, the entrance to the Acropolis. Between these two points is the opening of the Cave of Pan. Lysistrata, whose name means "She Who Disbands Armies," is an Athenian woman, and leader of the Athenian wives. She is walking up and down before her house, irritated that the other women she has invited have not yet arrived as they are so prone to doing everything late. Lysistrata notes that the women of Salamis would be especially interested to hear her speak as the sailors, and by extension their wives, had a comic reputation of sexual appetite. When Kalonike, another young Athenian wife, arrives, Lysistrata tells her she has asked the women to meet because of an extremely important mater involving the future of Greece. Indeed, as she tells Kalonike, the matter is so delicate and if such great importance, that "Greece's whole salvation / Depends entirely on the female sex." Lysistrata expects that the Acharnai women will be especially anxious to see her as it is a city vulnerable to Spartan ravages. Finally, the others begin to arrive. Among them are another Athenian named Myrrhine, who states that she had trouble getting dressed, the athletic-looking Lampito from Sparta, and three other young wives, all of whom are wearing short, revealing dresses.

When all are assembled, Lysistrata informs them that she has summoned this council of females to propose a plan for ending the Peloponnesian War because the war is depriving them of their husbands and their sexual pleasure. The situation, according to Lysistrata, is dire. "Not a glimmer of males—not a single adulterer left!" She tells the other women that they must refuse to make love to their husbands until the men agree to make peace. The women are shocked and upset by this proposal and many object to such a deprivation. Lysistrata accuses them of caring only for their sexual satisfaction. "The female sex! Sheer lustfulness, that's us! / No wonder they write such tragedies about us! / Our lives are simply full of sex and intrigue." However, when Lysistrata finally succeeds in convincing them of how well the plan will work, they give in, encouraging each other to keep resisting. "We've got to make them suffer in every way. / They'll soon give in: no husband can enjoy / A life of constant friction with his wife." She has arranged for the older women to seize the Acropolis, a citadel located in Athens, while they, the younger ones, make themselves attractive to their husbands. The women take an oath to dress beautifully and entice their husbands with the sole intention of refusing the men until they establish peace. Their agreement is finalized with the women drinking a toast to Divine Persuasion, a deity often cited in erotic contexts and long associated with Aphrodite, the goddess of love. Lampito returns to Sparta to organize the women there, while the others go to join the older women who have seized the Acropolis.

The old-men's half chorus now appears, struggling to carry logs and a brazier up the hillside with the intention of smoking "these women into submission" and ultimately driving them out of the Acropolis. Shortly thereafter, as the old men are building a fire, a chorus of old women enters carrying pots of water to extinguish the fire and they move at a pace considerably faster than their male counterparts. The two groups insult and threaten each other, and finally the women throw the water at the men, stating that they are exercising their freedom of speech and, by extension, their freedom of action. Then the Commissioner of Public Safety enters with some policemen. He scolds the women, "[f]emales again— spontaneous combustion of lust," and tries to force his way into the treasury to obtain money to pay rowers he has hired. Suddenly, however, a fully composed Lysistrata comes out and asks him what he wants. "Frankly, you don't need crowbars nearly so much as brains." When he orders the policemen to seize her, the women attack him with household items, and they retire in terror, with the

Commissioner exclaiming "[g]ross ineptitude. A sorry day for the Force."

Lysistrata then speaks proudly of the women who are going to save Greece despite the folly of the men. "We're not slaves; we're free-born Women, and when scorned we're full of fury." When the Magistrate remarks on the insolence of the women, Lysistrata replies that women have common sense, which men would do well to imitate. Finally, the women throw water at him, and he goes off. The chorus of old men then criticizes women for interfering in matters of state and warfare; asking of Zeus "[h]ow do we deal with this female zoo?" They are answered by the Chorus of Old Women, who speak of all that women have done for Athens, contributing their sons to the state, while the men merely waste its treasures. "Too many times, as we sat in the house, we'd hear that you'd done it again—manhandled another affair of state with your usual staggering incompetence."

Lysistrata emerges from the Acropolis, disheartened by the frailty of her colleagues. Desiring their husbands, the women are breaking their vows and trying to desert her. They pretend they must attend to their households. One women explains that she must get home because she has "some lovely Milesian wool in the house, and the moths will simply batter it to bits." And another goes so far as to hide a helmet under her clothes in order to pretend she is about to bear a child, to which Lysistrata responds by saying "[y]ou weren't pregnant yesterday." Lysistrata scolds and encourages them, and at last they return to the Acropolis. Seeing Kinesias, the husband of Myrrhine, approaching, Lysistrata orders Myrrhine to flirt with and provoke him and then turn away when he is enflamed with desire.

A delegation from Sparta then enters, hoping to make peace with Athens. They are inflamed with sexual desire and go to great lengths to hide their condition. "Behold our local Sons of the Soil, stretching their garments away from their groins, like wrestlers grappling with their plight. . . . An outbreak of epic proportions." One of the delegates speaks to Kinesias about their plight and Kinesias summons Lysistrata as the one who can effect peace. Lysistrata appears with her beautiful handmaid, Peace, who brings the Spartans before her mistress. Lysistrata addresses both Spartans and Athenians alike, admonishing them for having caused these dire circumstances. "With such a history of mutual benefits conferred and received, why are you fighting? Stop this wickedness!

Come to terms with each other!" The Choruses of Old Men and Old Women agree to quarrel no more, and together they sing of their hopes for peace. Soon ambassadors from Sparta enter, announcing that they have come to arrange for peace with Athens. Lysistrata comes out of the Acropolis, and the goddess Peace is brought in by the Machine. Lysistrata inveighs against war, pointing out the responsibility of both Athenians and Spartans. She invites the men to enter the Acropolis where they will feast with the women and vow to make peace and then to take their wives home. Soon a Spartan Chorus and an Athenian Chorus enter, dancing to the music of flutes. Lysistrata directs each of the Athenian delegates to "stand by his wife, each wife by her husband. Dance to the gods' glory, and thank them for a happy ending." Lysistrata and the women follow, and all sing and dance. ❧

# List of Characters in
## *Lysistrata*

*Speaking Characters:*

**Lysistrata:** leader of the Athenian wives

**Kalonike:** a young Athenian wife

**Myrrhine:** a young Athenian wife

**Lampito:** a Spartan wife

**Commissioner:** member of the Commission of Ten

**Kinesias:** Athenian citizen, husband of Myrrhine

**Herald:** Spartan messenger

**Spartan:** spokesman of the Spartan envoys who come to sue for peace

**Athenian:** leader of the Athenian envoys

**Old Men:** half-chorus of 12

**Women:** half chorus of 12

**Chorus:** incorporates the two half choruses (from line 1043 onward)

**Leader of Men:** of old men's half-chorus

**Leader of Women:** of women's half-chorus

**Leader:** of combined chorus

*Silent Characters:*

**Boiotian Woman**

**Korinthian Woman**

**Slave Girl:** of Lysistrata

**Archers:** slaves attending the Commissioner

**Baby:** child of Kinesias and Myrrhine

**Reconciliation:** naked female personification of peace

**Envoys:** official representatives of both Athens and Sparta

**Slaves:** various ❁

# Critical Views on
## *Lysistrata*

A. M. Bowie on Treatment of Women

[A. M. Bowie is the author of *The Poetic Dialect of Sappho and Alcaeus* (1981). In the chapter entitled "*Lysistrata,*" Bowie attributes Aristophanes' ambivalent treatment of women to the Greek ideology of his times.]

*Lysistrata* portrays the temporary imposition of a gynaecocracy on the city of Athens. Impossible as this was in practical terms, it was a concept frequently found in mythology and ritual. For the Athenians, the story of the Amazons was the best known local example, but they were also well acquainted with other famous versions, such as that of the Lemnian Women. Elements from these tales, along with others from a further, more historical example of the seizure of control by one who has no legitimate claim, are used in *Lysistrata* to present the women's actions in a negative light, but at the same time, there is a counterbalance of other, more positive models, such as the Thesmophoria, of times when women acted alone to the benefit of the city. This is a double presentation of events which we have seen in other plays.

This ambivalence in the play's representation of women reflects a similar ambivalence in their place in Greek ideology. In law, they were defined as 'incapable of a self-determined act, as almost . . . an un-person, outside the limits of those who constitute society's responsible and representative agents'. They had no formal political representation and were for a great part of the time confined to the *gunaikeion,* the women's quarters of the house. Marriage was conceived as the 'taming' of the wild young woman, as can be seen from the language used of it and the representations on vases of young, ephebic males 'hunting' the fleeing girl. Summarising his discussion of women in myth, Gould writes that

> male attitudes to women, and to themselves in relation to women, are marked by tension, anxiety and fear. Women are not part of, do not belong easily in, the male ordered world of the 'civilised' community; they have to be accounted for in other terms, and they threaten continu-

ally to overturn its stability or subvert its continuity, to break out of the place assigned to them by their partial incorporation within it. Yet they are essential to it: they are the producers and bestowers of wealth and children, the guarantors of due succession, the guardians of the *oikos* and its hearth. Men are their sons, and are brought up, as children, by them and among them. Like the earth and once-wild animals, they must be tamed and cultivated by men, but their wildness will out.

The idea of women in power is clearly marked in Greek ideology as abnormal, in that it occurs in mythology at times of crisis and in ritual at periods of the year which are themselves marked as abnormal. There is thus a similarity to the way 'slaves in power' is represented, which we discussed in connection with *Knights*. In the case of Argos after its defeat by Sparta, an oracle was fulfilled promising female domination over men; the women married the slaves, and the poetess Telesilla organised the defence of the city by the women. The myth was connected with the Hybristica festival in Argos, which commemorated the act of bravery by the women through the exchange of clothes between males and females. Similarly in Cumae, it was a woman, Xenocrite, who persuaded the young men, whom the tyrant Aristodemus had sent to a girlish existence in the country after murdering their fathers, to rise up and restore the city to normality. Women play comparable roles in the foundation-legends of Tarentum and Epizephyrian Locri. The case of the Lemnian Women will be discussed below.

The importance of women to the community was openly acknowledged in matters of religion: many priesthoods were held by women. The Thesmophoria, to be discussed in the next chapter, dramatised the ritual assumption by women of roles normally taken by men, in such areas as politics, sacrifice on behalf of the city, death and corruption. The whole festival celebrated women's role in the fertility of mankind and field.

—A. M. Bowie, "Lysistrata," *Aristophanes: Myth, Ritual and Comedy* (Cambridge and New York: Cambridge University Press, 1993): pp. 178–80.

[Jeffrey Henderson is the author of "Scribes, Scholars and Aristophanic Comedy" (1974) and *The Maculate Muse: Obscene Language in Attic Comedy* (1991). In the excerpt below from his article, "*Lysistrate:* The Play and Its Themes," Henderson discusses Aristophanes' Prologue as setting forth his skillful and unconventional employment of female heroines.]

In a genre where surprising and fantastic ideas are expected of the poet, where ordinary laws of cause and effect are often suspended from the start, we will not be amazed to discover that extravagant themes frequently demand much more from the limited potential of the Attic stage than even the most acrobatic of playwrights could hope to accommodate within the bounds of logic. This is part of the fun, and so it happens in *Lysistrate:* the women of Greece are to end a panhellenic war by employing traditional female attributes in new ways. The feat must be accomplished not only in the traditional female realm, the home, but also in the public realm of the men, both fighting men and politicians, and not only in Athens but in Sparta as well. All Greece is to be recalled from the madness of an ongoing war to those peaceful days when Athens and Sparta jointly led the Greek world. This emphasis on the Good Old Days was a familiar comic stance then as now; the desire for panhellenic unity, on the other hand, has a claim to be a particularly Aristophanic motif, since it is found scarcely at all in the fragments of other comic poets and does not appear prominently until the fourth century. All this is a tall order for a playwright who had only four actors, a Chorus, an orchestra, a small stage and a couple of doors on a wooden building. Yet the task is accomplished and in the realization of this complex and ambitious idea Aristophanes offers us a good opportunity to observe a master playwright manipulating his traditional medium to its fullest potential.

*Prologue (1–253)*

Lysistrate emerges from her house in the middle of a thought. We are not told the time of day but it soon appears that it is no longer early in the morning (60). Lysistrate has been waiting for women to arrive and complains that if the women had been invited to some festival of Dionysos, Pan or Aphrodite Genetyllis the crowd would have been impassable. As it is no one is yet here. These opening words tell us two things. (1) Lysistrate is the organizer of a meeting for women that is not of the usual (i.e. festive) kind. (2) She feels herself to be superior to the others in that she can think of an activity that does not fall into the category of revelry, drinking, sex and childbirth (for these are the activities associated with the deities mentioned and traditionally said by men to be the sole preoccupations of women). Lysistrate assumes a role traditionally assumed to be a male prerogative: calling a meeting, possessing will-power and entertaining ideas rather than physical drives.

The audience is likely to have been surprised to hear this and indeed to see a woman in the first place. Although heroines had long been customary in tragedy (since they were prominent in heroic myth) they were a rarity in comedy. In Aristophanes' earlier plays we have seen nothing like this. The only women who have appeared before were the odd market woman or minor goddess. A dozen or so Old Comedies of which only titles and/or fragments remain can be said to have had female Choruses, but only Pherekrates' *Tyrannis* can be said possibly to have had a female protagonist, though that is uncertain. The idea of staging an intrigue-comedy with a heroine may well be original with Aristophanes.

> —Jeffrey Henderson, "*Lysistrata:* The Play and Its Themes," *Aristophanes: Essays in Interpretation: Yale Classical Studies* vol. XXVI: pp. 168–70.

## Hans-Joachim Newiger on the Conditions in Athens

[Hans-Joachim Newiger is the author of "Hofmannsthals Elektra und die griechische Tragodie" (1969) and *Metapher und Allegorie: Studien zu Aristophanes* (1957). In the excerpt below from his article, "War and Peace in the Comedy of Aristophanes," Newiger discusses the perilous condition in Athens during the time in which *Lysistrata* was written and performed.]

Ten years later in 411, four years after the second outbreak of the war and in a time of great tribulation, Aristophanes produced Lysistrata. In the autumn of 413 Athens had not only lost vast numbers of troops in Sicily, almost her entire fleet and her most capable generals, but since the spring of 413 the Spartans, on the advice of the turncoat Alcibiades, had established themselves under King Agis in Decelea, only fifteen miles from Athens, and from there maintained continuous control over the Attic countryside. ⟨. . .⟩

But Athens continued the war with unbelievable obstinacy. Through the introduction of new tariffs and the expenditure of her last financial reserves she built a new fleet, and in the autumn of 412, at approximately the time when Aristophanes was putting the final touches on *Lysistrata,* over one hundred ships, based on Samos, stood off the Ionian coast of Asia Minor. In Athens, the saying resounded just as it had fourteen years earlier, 'Let the war continue!' The women at the beginning of *Lysistrata* also use this saying as they hear what they must do to end the war.

Athens' perilous external situation went hand-in-hand with an extremely threatening domestic situation. The military failures of the democratic administration gave the oligarchs their opportunity to restrict and perhaps even eliminate the democracy which since Pericles' death had become more and more radical and whose leaders were the driving force behind the continuation of the war. The oligarchs were also intent on a settlement with Sparta for reasons of internal politics. The establishment of a new governing body of ten probouloi (to which the so-called 'Councillor' appearing in the first part of *Lysistrata* belongs) represented the first restriction of the democracy, for these probouloi curtailed the rights of the prytaneis and the Council; Sophocles, incidentally, was one of them. These tensions existed even in the fleet on Samos, and from there the oligarchic rebellion, which followed a few months after the performance of *Lysistrata,* gained significant momentum. Thus the conception and performance of this comedy took place in a constantly worsening situation which threatened Athens (and this must be stressed) in both the internal and external political spheres.

The greater universality with which Aristophanes now treats the old theme of war and peace stems to some extent from the tendency of all the extant plays after *Birds* to be less limited to a particular time and situation. The explanation is, however, also to be sought in the political situation, which would scarcely have tolerated any partisanship on the part of the poet. ⟨...⟩

A plot summary will show how the old theme of war and peace is handled here. Under the leadership of Lysistrata, married women from Athens as well as Sparta, Boeotia and Corinth meet and form a conspiracy, after Lysistrata has persuaded them that the only plausible method of obtaining peace must be a refusal to perform their conjugal duties. That this ticklish theme is treated coarsely and explicitly is quite understandable, given the nature of Old Comedy. In particular, the women doubt their own ability to hold out, but finally take a pledge not to surrender themselves to their husbands willingly, but in fact to excite them through provocative behavior. Employed in all the warring states simultaneously, this method has an immediate success.

> —Hans-Joachim Newiger, "War and Peace in the Comedy of Aristophanes," *Aristophanes: Essays in Interpretation: Yale Classical Studies* vol. XXVI: pp. 228–30.

## Danny L. Smith on the Tragic Political Background

> [Danny L. Smith is the author of *To Be Once in Doubt: Certainty and the Marriage of Minds in "Othello"* (1989). In the excerpt below from his article, "War and the Body in *Lysistrata:* Marriage and the Family Under Siege," Smith discusses the play's latent tragic political background within the ostensibly comic and ridiculous.]

Presented for the Lenaea in 411 B.C. at that bleak period of the Peloponnesian War—the Athenian fleet destroyed in Sicily, the final defeat at Aegospotami only seven years away—*Lysistrata* has every right to be a polemic for peace and an apology for family life. As a comedy it cannot bluntly do this, of course. While it has a tragic air about it because of the perilous circumstances of the war, it has as a comedy an affectionate witty charm in its treatment of the ridiculous, the bawdy, and the improbable. For the Greek audience (unlike the modern audience) the play's bawdy wit is inseparable from its tragic historical context: one hinges upon the other.

The desperate situation with the war and the absence of the men produced a tension in both the *oikos* and the *polis* the urgency of which is metaphorically portrayed as the growing sexual tension between Athenian and Spartan husbands and wives. As unrequited needs grow more desperate, this tension is felt even by the strong and idealistic Lysistrata herself when she emphatically cries: ⟨. . .⟩ "To sum it up in a word, we're dying to get laid".

This bawdiness serves to point out some serious facts about bodies, families and wars. Like most of Aristophanes' work *Lysistrata* is, as Joyce would put it, jocoserious: comic with a serious side. It is the story of a strong and beautiful Athenian wife, Lysistrata, her name meaning Disbander of Armies, who in league with representative wives of the chief belligerent Grecian cities—friend and foe— conspires to end the Peloponnesian War by proposing that the women deny their men (and themselves) sexual intercourse. In conference the women rebel at such a drastic measure, but Lysistrata finds her first ray of hope in her worthiest ally, the Spartan Lampito, whose name has the appropriate connotation of torch-bearer, shining or lustrous one.

Appreciating the difficulty of the strategy, Lampito nonetheless senses the possible kinship between eros and thymos; thus her reference to Menelaus' giving up the sword at the sight of Helen's breasts seems to win the day. The Athenian and Spartan desire peace equally. These strong enemies, potentially strong allies can reunite Helas if their eros can be redirected toward proper, familial concerns.

So it is that Lysistrata and Lampito, allied, successfully persuade the rest of the women—dismissing with a bawdy joke the intrusive but starkly real possibility that the men might simply leave or ignore them. Together the women swear to deny the men sexual favors while exciting them at every opportunity, to be unresponsive if forced, and to thus induce them to sue for the armistice. ⟨. . .⟩

The women have won, all male delegates of both sides being physically incapacitated. The old men, wet and naked from their dousing, are comforted, clothed, kissed and reconciled; and the leader of the hemichorus of old women removes from the eye of the leader of the old men a biting insect, the figurative source and symbol of his anger. Then the younger men are led off, willingly by the hand—or if unwilling then by the other appropriate handle—to negotiate their concessions, Spartan and Athenian together. At this point we see "Peace" or "Reconciliation" led in, personified by a beautiful naked lady, and the negotiators, enraptured now with peace, indeed lustful for her, chart their disputed hills and valleys on her body, the topography continually punned as anatomy. ⟨. . .⟩

⟨. . .⟩ Kenneth Dover cites the fact that sexual activity on the Akropolis would have been sacrilege, that the play must end on a note other than satisfaction of the pressing need. My point is that the need *is* satisfied—allegorically. Everything in the play leads to the conclusion that private and political worlds finally consummate a union.

> —Danny L. Smith, "War and the Body in *Lysistrata:* Marriage and the Family Under Siege," *Allegory Revisited: Ideals of Mankind* (Dordrecht: Boston and London: Kluwer Academic Publishers, 1994): pp. 65–67.

## ALAN H. SOMMERSTEIN ON THE TURBULENCE IN ATHENS

[Alan H. Sommerstein is the editor of Aeschylus' *Eumenides* (1989) and an editor of *Education in Greek Fiction* (1997). In the excerpt below from his translation and introduction to *Lysistrata,* Sommerstein discusses the turbulent political situation in Athens.]

*Lysistrata* was produced for Aristophanes by his old collaborator Callistratus at one of the dramatic festivals held early in 411 B.C.; the ancient headnote (Hypothesis) to the play does not specify which festival, but it is now generally agreed that it was the Lenaea, which that year fell in what by the Julian calendar would be the first half of February.

At this time the political and military situation of Athens was, in almost every respect, very bad. Although it was over a year since the annihilation of the Sicilian expedition, Athens had hardly begun to recover from that disaster. Many of her most important allies were in revolt; the Peloponnesians were lending them energetic assistance; the Persian governors in western Asia Minor, Tissaphernes and Pharnabazus, were actively seeking to bring the Athenian-allied cities on the Asian mainland back under Persian rule, and engaging in negotiations for an alliance with Sparta; meanwhile in Attica itself the enemy garrison at Deceleia continued to dominate the country-side, effectively confining the Athenians to the Athens-Peiraeus forti-fied zone and cutting them off from their agricultural land and from the silver mines of Laureium. ⟨. . .⟩ Many Athenians must have been as surprised as most other Greeks were that at the end of 412 they were still alive and fighting; and as was soon to be shown, few if any could see a way to bring the war to a victorious or even a tolerable end, unless some new source not only of naval and military but above all of financial support could be found. ⟨. . .⟩

⟨. . .⟩ Thus so far as most Athenians were concerned the war was simply going on as usual, and not going very well; it was their ene-mies who were making persistent attempts to enlist Persia as an ally, and there was no knowing whether they might not before long succeed, with catastrophic consequences for Athens. Early defeat was a very real possibility, and at best Athens could only look for-ward to an indefinite prolongation of the war; peace could only come either by Athenian surrender (which was unthinkable) or by a miracle from the world of fantasy, the world in which Old Comedy dwells. And in *Lysistrata* the miracle is made to take place. *Lysistrata* does not advocate the termination of the war by an Athenian initiative: such an initiative had, in the existing situation, no chance of success except on terms that even the most antidemo-cratic, pro-Spartan factions at Athens would never dare to accept—as the Four Hundred were to discover a few months later. Rather it dreams a dream: a dream of the women of Greece uniting to force their male-governed communities to bury the hatchet and resume the old friendship in which Athens and Sparta had come to each other's aid in time of need and defeated the Persian invader together—a work of liberation which, even as *Lysistrata* was being written, Persia was beginning to undo.

The play is built around two separate schemes devised by Lysistrata, and put into effect by different groups of women under her direction, to force male Greece to end the war. The first, and the more prominent in the play as a whole, is the boycotting of sexual relations. This campaign is prosecuted by the younger married women of Athens and Sparta such as Calonice, Myrrhine and Lampito. Its effects on the men become manifest for the first time in the Cinesias-Myrrhine scene, which is immediately followed by the first moves towards negotiations for peace. Its prime visible symbol is the erect phallus, which is little used in Aristophanes' other plays but which in *Lysistrata* 829–1188 is worn by every male who comes on the scene (except the old men of the chorus). Its presiding deity is Aphrodite.

But once the sexual strike has been proposed, accepted and sworn to, there is no further explicit reference to it until the second half of the play, and from 240 to 613 the action centres wholly on the other scheme: the seizure by the Athenian women of the Acropolis (where the financial reserves of the state were kept) with the object of denying Athens the resources to fight on. Unlike the sexual strike, this is a purely Athenian action. It is carried out in the first instance by "the over-age women" who cannot take part in the strike since their days of sexual activity are assumed to be over; though once they have occupied the Acropolis, the younger Athenian women soon join them there. The dramatic climaxes of this aspect of the action are two assaults on the Acropolis, first by the old men of the chorus and then by the Magistrate and his assistants.

—Alan H. Sommerstein, *Lysistrata* (Warminster: Aris & Phillips Ltd., 1990): pp. 1, 3–4.

## LAUREN K. TAAFFE ON FEMININE SOLIDARITY

[Lauren K. Taaffe is the author of *Aristophanes and Women*. In the excerpt below from the chapter entitled "Women as Women, Men as Men: *Lysistrata*," Taaffe discusses the theme of feminine solidarity.]

The younger wives' sex strike and their husbands' subsequent capitulation, the older women's occupation of the Athenian treasury and their physical victory over a band of decrepit and angry old men, and certainly the charisma of its eponymous heroine have all combined to make *Lysistrata* a favorite among scholars and students alike. Its frank recognition of heterosexuality titillates and amuses. Once bowdlerized, the play is now often seen as a statement of feminine solidarity and of universal truths about war, peace, and the battle of the sexes. On top of that, it satisfies, as no other Aristophanic play does, an audience's desire for cohesiveness and clarity: its sustained plot has a beginning, a middle, and an end.

*Lysistrata* turns upon clearly determined stereotypes of sex and gender. Its humor relies on role reversal to befuddle audience expectations. That humor is rather tendentious, for as the women deny their sexual urges in order to distract their husbands from the war, they become, more and more, emblems of a male vision of femininity. ⟨. . .⟩

Women have significant speaking roles in *Lysistrata,* which is the earliest extant ancient Greek comic play to feature women in central roles and possibly the first play of its kind altogether, although this cannot be determined for certain. That the first extant Attic comedy with women as main characters did not appear until 411 BCE, relatively late in the history of ancient Greek drama, has caught the attention of only a few critics. Most mention the phenomenon, praise Aristophanes' comic genius, and move on to other issues, arguably skeptical and interested in other matters. In contrast to tragedy, for which there are many earlier fifth-century female characters both major and minor, the only females found in comedy prior to *Lysistrata* were personifications (e.g. comedy in Kratinos' *Pytine;* Opora and Theoria in *Peace*), mythological figures (e.g. Iris in *Birds*), wives and daughters of male characters, with relatively few lines to speak (e.g. Dikaiopolis' wife and daughter in *Acharnians;* Trygaeus' daughters in *Peace*), or mute flute girls (e.g. Philocleon's companion at the end of *Wasps*). ⟨. . .⟩

## STAGING THE COMIC WOMAN

The initial scene of *Lysistrata,* in which the heroine outlines her plan, does much to establish one layer of the play's metatheatricality.

Lysistrata's proposal requires that the women borrow the most basic technique of theater: role-playing. Lysistrata requests that the women act to stop the war because the men's actions have failed to do so. Since public policy is traditionally the exclusive domain of men, the women here take the places of men in public life. In theatrical terms, they are acting or playing male roles.

Lysistrata's proposed scheme has a twist to it, however. The roles these women play entail their acting more like women than they already do. In stepping into the roles of men, they will assume the passive roles of women: as ideal images of sexuality in the eyes of their husbands. In theatrical terms, the women will represent women as part of their taking on of the political roles of men. Then the plot twists again. The women's active (or acted) passivity entices its intended audience, their husbands, who approach with extended phalloi and in increasing discomfort. The husbands' appearance displays a dramatically exaggerated masculinity just as these men are stepping into the fictional and symbolic roles of women, as creatures physically representative of home-bound fertility, needful of and overtly preoccupied with sex, willing to relinquish control of public policy, and eager to return to the confines of home and marriage.

•In the final analysis, we might describe Lysistrata's plan as a play in which women enact the roles of men by playing the parts of 'women' and men enact the roles of women by playing the parts of 'men'. This play is resolved when the middle, role-playing, level of character is eliminated and the super-feminine women reunite with their super-masculine men and recreate ideal marriages.

—Lauren K. Taaffe, "Women as Women, Men as Men: *Lysistrata*," *Aristophanes and Women* (London and New York: Routledge, 1993): pp. 48–49, 51–52.

## CEDRIC H. WHITMAN ON LYSISTRATA'S FEMININE NATURE

[Cedric H. Whitman is one of the authors of *Euripides and the Full Circle of Myth* (1974) and *The Heroic Paradox:*

*Essays on Homer, Sophocles and Aristophanes* (1982). In the excerpt below from the chapter entitled "War Between the Sexes" Whitman discusses the decidedly feminine nature of Lysistrata and attributes her success in transforming society to that femininity.]

The *Birds,* with its detachment and its view of Athens under the guise of a kind of comic whole, was a performance which could not be repeated. One could always return to the parts, however, and in the plays of 411 Aristophanes returns to more confined issues for the sources of fantasy. But "one cannot cross the same river twice": Athens had changed, and Aristophanes had changed. The theme is familiar: peace, conceived not negatively as the mere absence of war, but as a set of concrete images, focusing in this case around the central image of sex. But the mood is far different from that of the *Acharnians* or the *Peace,* which celebrated the confident and essentially victorious city of the twenties, when the polis, and especially this particular polis, was its own rounded world, and, despite its increasing imperialism, its alienation of the individual, and its tendency toward bureaucratic atrophy, a structure to take pride in, as the natural social order. In 411 there was little of this feeling left. ⟨. . .⟩ In the earlier plays of Aristophanes the city had been blandly subsumed as an integral, given fact. The outspoken criticism of policies, politicians, and officials had been a symptom of basic confidence in the democratic scheme, whether or not one believes that that criticism was offered with serious intent. ⟨. . .⟩ But it is in part attributable also to the broader view of things which characterizes Aristophanes' later work; if the full-blown symbolism of the *Birds* could not be repeated, neither could it be totally forgotten, and in his later plays, except for the heart-felt curses on Cleophon in the *Frogs,* the political aspect expresses itself very seldom in personal attack, and more in general figures and actions which respond symbolically to the state of the city.

The clearest examples of this method, as will be seen, are the figures of Dionysus, Aeschylus, and Euripides in the *Frogs.* Lysistrata too belongs with them, in that she is, so to speak, a collective, representing not only women in general, but also a historical and political view of Athens, and perhaps even something of the Panhellenic ideal. But she is far from being pure allegory, for she is also an individual whose personality is strikingly clear, and like the earlier protagonists of Aristophanes she possesses a heroic decisiveness which at once isolates her and permits her to subdue society to her ends. She does not, however, transcend society; she transforms it by restoring peace, while she herself stays within it. For this reason, perhaps, there is little or nothing of the motif of apotheosis. Lysistrata is not, in fact, a grotesque figure, in the sense in which the word has been used in this book, for she does not possess the animal and divine dimensions—except, perhaps, in a different sense and one which befits the nature of her fantastic effort. ⟨. . .⟩ Lysistrata is a woman, with a woman's purpose and a woman's methods, and when her purpose is accomplished, she retires with becoming modesty, presumably into the arms of her own husband. It is sometimes stated that she is masculine in temper and manner, and as evidence the Spartan's remark about "Lysistratus" is adduced. This is a serious mistake, however; the whole point of the action lies in femininity and the desirable charms which Lysistrata and her accomplices withhold. She is without question strong-minded, but whoever considers that quality a strictly masculine one is in error, not to say danger. It is clear from the beginning, where Calonice tells her that frowning does not become her, to the end, where the leaders of all Greece are "caught by her love-charm," that Lysistrata is young and pretty. The role can be played properly only by an actress of singular grace and charm.

—Cedric H. Whitman, "War Between the Sexes." In *Aristophanes and the Comic Hero* (Cambridge, Massachusetts: Harvard University Press, 1964): pp. 200–2.

# Works by Aristophanes

*Banqueters* (427 B.C.)

*Babylonians* (426 B.C.)

*Acharnians* (425 B.C.)

*Knights* (424 B.C.)

*Clouds* (423 B.C.)

*Wasps* (422 B.C.)

*Peace* (421 B.C.)

*Amphiaraus* (414 B.C.)

*Birds* (414 B.C.)

*Lysistrata* (411 B.C.)

*Plutus* (first ) (408 B.C.)

*Frogs* (405 B.C.)

*Ecclesiazusae* (392 B.C.)

*Plutus* (second) (388 B.C.)

*Aiolosikon* (after 388 B.C.)

*Cocalus* (after 388 B.C.)

# Works About
# Aristophanes

Anastaplo, George. *The Thinker as Artist: From Homer to Plato & Aristotle.* Athens: Ohio University Press, 1997.

Anderson, Carl A. *Athena's Epithets: Their Structural Significance in the Plays of Aristophanes.* Stuttgart: Teubner, 1995.

Bassi, Karen. *Acting Like Men: Gender, Drama, and Nostalgia in Ancient Greece.* Ann Arbor: University of Michigan Press, 1998.

Boegehold, Alan L. *When a Gesture Was Expected: A Selection of Examples from Archaic and Clasical Greek Literature.* Princeton, New Jersey: Princeton University Press, 1999.

Breyfogle, Todd and David Green. *Literary Imagination, Ancient and Modern: Essays in Honor of David Grene.* Chicago: University of Chicago Press, 1999.

Carey, C. "Comic Ridicule and Democracy." In R. Osborne and S. Hornblower (eds.), *Ritual, Finance, Politics: Athenian Democratic Accounts Presented to David Lewis.* Oxford, 1994: 69–83.

Cartledge, Paul. *Aristophanes and His Theatre of the Absurd.* London: Bristol Classical Press, 1992.

Chambers, Mortimer. *Text & Tradition: Studies in Greek History & Historiography in Honor of Mortimer Chambers.* Claremont, California: Regina Books, 1999.

Claeys, Gregory. *The Utopia Reader.* New York: New York University Press, 1999.

Colvin, Stephen. *Dialect in Aristophanes and the Politics of Language in Ancient Greek Literature.* Oxford: Clarendon Press, 1999.

Cook, Eleanor. *Against Coercion: Games Poets Play.* California: Stanford University Press, 1998.

Dearden, C. W. *The Stage of Aristophanes.* London: University of London, Athlone Press; Atlantic Highlands, New Jersey: Humanities Press, 1976.

DeHaven-Smith, Lance. *Foundations of Representative Democracy.* New York: Peter Lang, 1999.

Dickey, Eleanor. *Greek Forms of Address: From Herodotus to Lucian.* New York: Clarendon Press, 1996.

Dobrov, Gregory W. *The City of Comedy: Society and Representation in Athenian Drama.* Chapel Hill, North Carolina: University of North Carolina Press, 1997.

————. *Beyond Aristophanes: Transition and Diversity in Greek Comedy.* Atlanta, Georgia: Scholars Press, 1995.

Dover, Kenneth James. *Aristophanic Comedy.* Berkeley: University of California Press, 1972.

Dutton, Dana Ferrin. *Self and Society in Aristophanes.* Washington, D.C.: University Press of America, 1980.

————. *Ancient Comedy: The War of the Generations.* New York: Twayne; Toronto: Maxwell Macmillan Canada; New York: Maxwell Macmillan International, 1993.

Ehrenberg, Victor. *The People of Aristophanes: A Sociology of Old Attic Comedy.* New York: Schocken Books, 1962.

Euben J. Peter. *Corrupting Youth: Political Education, Democratic Culture, and Political Theory.* Princeton, New Jersey: Princeton University Press, 1997.

Finnegan, Rachel. *Women in Aristophanes.* Amsterdam: Adolf M. Hakkert, 1995.

Fisher, Raymond K. *Aristophanes' Clouds: Purpose and Technique.* Amsterdam: Adolf M. Hakkert, 1984.

Griffiths, Alan, ed. *Stage Directions: Essays in Ancient Drama in Honour of E. W. Handley.* London: Institute of Classical Studies, 1995.

Hair, Donald S. Robert. *Browning's Language.* Toronto; Buffalo, New York: University of Toronto Press 1999.

Harvey, F. David, John Wilkins and Kenneth J. Dover. *The Rivals of Aristophanes: Studies in Athenian Old Comedy.* London: Duckworth and the Classical Press of Wales, 2000.

Heath, Malcolm. *Political Comedy in Aristophanes.* Gottingen: Vandenhoeck & Ruprecht, 1987.

Henderson, Jeffrey, ed. *Aristophanes: Essays in Interpretation.* Cambridge, England, and New York: Cambridge University Press, 1980.

Kaimio, M. "Comic Violence in Aristophanes. *Arctos* 24 (1990): 47–72.

Kass, Amy A., and Leon Kass. *Wing to Wing, Oar to Oar: Readings on Courting and Marrying.* Notre Dame, Indiana: University of Notre Dame Press, 2000.

Littlefield, David J., ed. *Twentieth Century Interpretations of* The Frogs: *A Collection of Critical Essays.* Englewood Cliffs, New Jersey: Prentice-Hall, 1968.

MacDowell, Douglas M. *Aristophanes and Athens: An Introduction to the Plays.* Oxford and New York: Oxford University Press, 1995.

McLeish, Kenneth. *The Theatre of Aristophanes.* London: Thames and Hudson, 1980.

Munn, Mark Henderson. *The School of History: Athens in the Age of Socrates.* Los Angeles and London: University of California Press, 2000.

Newman, Jay. *Inauthentic Culture and Its Philosophical Critics.* Montreal: McGill-Queen's University Press, 1997.

Newman, Rafael Francis David Amadeus. *The Visible God: Staging the History of Money.* Lanham: University Press of America, 1999.

Ober, Josiah. *Political Dissent in Democratic Athens: Intellectual Critics of Popular Rule.* Princeton, New Jersey: Princeton University Press, 1998.

O'Bryhim, Shawn and George Fredric Franko. *Greek and Roman Comedy: Translations and Interpretations of Four Representative Plays.* Austin: University of Texas Press, 2001.

Peradotto, John. *Contextualizing Classics: Ideology, Performance, Dialogue: Essays in Honor of John J. Peradotto.* Lanham, Maryland: Rowman & Littlefield, 1999.

Reckford, Kenneth J. *Aristophanes' Old-and-New Comedy.* Chapel Hill: University of North Carolina Press, 1987.

Rosen, Ralph Mark. *Old Comedy and the Iambographic Tradition.* Atlanta, Georgia: Scholars Press, 1988.

Russo, Carlo Ferdinando. *Aristophanes: An Author for the Stage.* Trans. by Kevin Wren. London and New York: Routledge, 1994.

Russon, John Edward. *Retracing the Platonic Text.* Evanston, Illinois: Northwestern University Press, 2000.

Segal, Erich. *Oxford Readings in Aristophanes.* New York: Oxford University Press, 1996.

Scharffenberger, Elizabeth Watson. *The Motif of Nostalgic Idealization in Aristophanes.* Ph.D. thesis: Columbia University, 1988.

Silk, M. S. *Aristophanes and the Definition of Comedy.* New York: Oxford University Press, 2000.

Sommerstein Alan H. and Catherine Atherton. *Education in Greek Fiction.* Bari: Levante, 1997.

Tejera, Victorino. *Plato's Dialogues One by One: A Dialogical Interpretation.* Lanham, Maryland: University Press of America, 1999.

Thorley, John. *Athenian Democracy.* London and New York: Routledge, 1996.

Titchener Frances B. *The Eye Expanded: Life and the Arts in Greco-Roman Antiquity.* Berkeley: University of California Press, 1999.

Van Steen, Gonda Aline Hector. *Venom in Verse.* Princeton, New Jersey: Princeton University Press, 2000.

Verstraete, Ginette. *Fragments of the Feminine Sublime in Friedrich Schlegel and James Joyce.* Albany: State University of New York Press, 1998.

Vickers, Michael J. *Pericles on Stage: Political Comedy in Aristophanes' Early Plays.* Austin: University of Texas Press, 1997.

West, Thomas G. and Grace Starry West. *Four Texts on Socrates: Plato's* Euthyphro, Apology, *and* Crito, *and Aristophanes'* Clouds. Ithaca: Cornell University Press, 1984.

Zeitlin, Froma I. *Playing the Other: Gender and Society in Classical Greek Literature.* Chicago: University of Chicago Press, 1996.

# Index of
# Themes and Ideas

*ACHARNIANS,* 46, 50, 58, 60, 70, 81–82, 105

ARISTOPHANES, 19–32; and Bakhtin's definition of carnivalesque, 27–29; biography of, 13–16; and comedy in Western literature, 23–24; comic and conversational language of, 21–22; English response to, 29–32; and literary aspects of comedies, 25–27

*BIRDS,* 33–50, 58, 60, 85, 100, 107; absurd in, 15; and Aeschylean tragedy, 24; birds in, 33–34, 35, 36, 39–41, 44–46, 47–50; characters in, 37–38; choral songs in, 14; Cloudcuckooland in, 34; comparison of animal and human behaviors in, 41–42; critical views on, 10–12, 39–50; escapism in, 39, 40–42, 47–48; Euelpides in, 10, 33, 34, 37, 42, 46, 49; Hoopoe in, 10, 33–34, 37, 39, 44–45, 47; Kinesias in, 35–36; opening of, 33–34, 45–46; phantastic elements in, 43–45; Pisthetairos in, 10, 11–12, 33, 34–35, 36, 37, 39, 40, 42, 46, 47, 49, 50, 70; plot summary of, 33–36; politics and myth in, 45–46; Prometheus in, 11–12, 36, 37; sexuality in, 49–50; symbolism of birds in, 39–41, 47–50; as today's Cloudcuckooland, 10–12; and true birth of comedy, 48–50; women in, 105; Zeus in, 36, 50

*CLOUDS,* 46, 51–70; Aeschylus in, 25, 56; carnivalesque in, 29; characters in, 57; chorus of clouds in, 40, 54–55, 56, 58, 60, 63–65, 66, 67–69; critical views in, 58–70; Euripides in, 25, 26, 82; Just Discourse in, 55; justice in, 65–67; literary aspects in, 25–26, 58–59; negative ending of, 62–63, 66, 70; opening of, 53; Pheidippides in, 15, 53, 55, 56, 57, 60–61, 62, 64, 66, 69; plot summary of, 51–56; as political satire, 63–65; as satire on sophist teachers, 51–52, 53–56, 58–59, 69–70; and Shelley's "The Cloud," 67–69; Socrates in, 15, 25, 52–53, 54, 55, 56, 57, 59, 60, 64, 66, 69, 70; Sophocles in, 30; Strepsiades in, 25, 53–55, 56, 57, 60–61, 62, 63, 64, 66, 69–70; Unjust Discourse in, 29, 55, 69, 70

*ECCLESIAZUSAE,* 60

*FROGS, THE,* 58, 71–88, 107; Aeacus in, 73, 74; Aeschylus in, 25, 71, 74–75, 76, 78, 80–82, 83, 85, 107; carnivalesque in, 28; characters in, 76; chorus of frogs in, 72–73, 74, 75, 80, 83, 85; critical views on, 77–88; Dionysus in, 15, 26, 71, 72–74, 75, 76, 77–78, 79–80, 82, 83, 85–88, 107; Euripides in, 25, 26–27, 71, 72, 74–75, 76, 78, 81–84, 85,

107; Heracles in, 26, 72, 76, 79, 85; literary aspects in, 25, 26–27, 71, 82–84; as metacriticism, 77–78; and place in Greek literature, 84–86; plot summary of, 71–75; Pluto in, 74, 76, 80; poets as teachers in, 25; sexuality in, 13; staging in, 79–80; Xanthias in, 71, 72, 73, 74, 76, 79, 80, 83, 85–86

*KNIGHTS,* 46, 58, 60, 81, 96

*LYSISTRATA,* 60, 69, 85, 89–108; characters in, 93; chorus of old men in, 90, 91, 92, 102, 104, 105; chorus of old women in, 90, 91, 92, 102; critical views on, 95–108; Kalonike in, 89, 93, 104, 108; Kinesias in, 91, 104; Lampito in, 89, 90, 93, 101, 104; Lysistrata in, 70, 89–92, 93, 97–98, 100, 101, 104, 105–8; Myrrhine in, 89, 91, 93, 104; plot summary of, 89–92; and political background, 14, 89–90, 98–104; prologue in, 97–98; sexuality in, 89–90, 91, 92, 98, 100, 101–2, 104, 105, 106; staging of, 105–6; women in, 15, 89–92, 95–97, 98, 100, 101–2, 103–8

MIDDLE COMEDY, 17, 84

NEW COMEDY, 17, 24, 30, 31, 43, 84

OLD COMEDY, 29, 30, 31, 33, 42, 43, 45, 53, 60, 73, 83–84, 87, 89, 100, 103

*PEACE,* 46, 60, 70, 82, 105

*PLUTUS,* 14, 17, 32

*THESMOPHORIAZUSAE,* 81, 82, 85

*WASPS,* 39–40, 46, 60, 70, 81, 105

*WEALTH,* 46